CARIBOO GOLD RUSH

The Stampede that Made BC

EDITED BY ART DOWNS

VICTORIA · VANCOUVER · CALGARY

Heritage House Publishing Company Ltd.
heritagehouse.ca

Library and Archives Canada Cataloguing in Publication
Downs, Art, 1924–
    Cariboo gold rush: the stampede that made BC / Art Downs.

(Amazing stories)
Includes bibliographical references and index.
Issued also in electronic formats.
ISBN 978-1-927527-19-1

1. Cariboo (BC: Regional district)—Gold discoveries. 2. British Columbia—History—1849–1871.
I. Title. II. Series: Amazing stories (Victoria, BC)

FC3822.5.D59 2013   971.1'75   C2013-900040-2

Series editor: Lesley Reynolds
Proofreader: Liesbeth Leatherbarrow

Cover photo: The Discovery of Gold on Williams Creek in 1861, from a painting by John Innes and
reproduced courtesy Native Sons of British Columbia, Post No. 2.

MIX
Paper from
responsible sources
FSC
www.fsc.org   FSC® C016245

The interior of this book was produced on 30% post-consumer recycled
paper, processed chlorine free and printed with vegetable-based inks.

Heritage House acknowledges the financial support for its publishing program from the Government
of Canada through the Canada Book Fund (CBF), Canada Council for the Arts and the province of
British Columbia through the British Columbia Arts Council and the Book Publishing Tax Credit.

 Canadian   Patrimoine
Heritage   canadien

Canada Council   Conseil des Arts
for the Arts   du Canada

 BRITISH COLUMBIA
ARTS COUNCIL

17 16 15 14 13 1 2 3 4 5
Printed in Canada

Contents

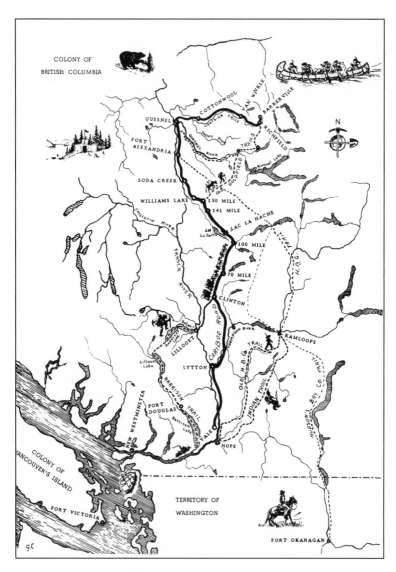

The route of the Cariboo Wagon Road in 1865, with some of the main Hudson's Bay Company trails and early miners' routes to the goldfields. At the beginning of the rush each party found its own way to the creeks, resulting in many trails through the wilderness.

GWEN LEWIS

Preface

ORIGINALLY PUBLISHED IN 1987 and edited by Art Downs, *Cariboo Gold Rush* explores the dramatic history of the gold rush that made BC. In the present edition, five chapters describing the 1858 stampede to the Fraser River and subsequent discovery of the gold-laden creeks in the Cariboo Mountains are excerpted from *British Columbia from the Earliest Times to the Present, Volume Two*. This massive series on BC's earliest history was published in 1914, its authors Judge F.W. Howay and Provincial Librarian-Archivist E.O.S. Scholefield.

Judge Howay (1867–1943) was born in New Westminster. He taught school in Ladner before switching to law, was appointed to the County Court in 1907 and spent 30 years as a judge. His career as a judge and an author resulted in many awards and appointments, including chairman of the Historic Sites and Monuments Board of Canada and president of the Canadian Historical Society. Mount Judge Howay, a peak in the Stave Lake area, near Vancouver, was named in his honour by the Canadian government.

E.O.S. Scholefield (1875–1919) was born in England but educated in Victoria. In 1894, he joined the staff of the Provincial Library and began a distinguished career. In 1898 he became Provincial Librarian and in 1910 also Provincial Archivist. In a few years he transformed the Provincial Library, adding some 50,000 titles in the first 14 years he held office. He was especially interested in Northwest history, obtaining many collections of manuscripts, books and newspapers for the BC Archives. Scholefield was only 44 when he died after a long illness. Many people felt his illness in part resulted from the long hours he spent as custodian of BC's Provincial Library and Archives.

The final chapter of the book gives a vivid, eyewitness view of Cariboo life from the journal of Dr. Walter B. Cheadle, first published in 1931 as *Cheadle's Journal of a Trip across Canada 1862–63*, and republished in 2010 by TouchWood Editions, with an introduction by Stephen R. Bown. In 1863, Cheadle and Lord Viscount Milton, the sixth Earl Fitzwilliam, became the first tourists to the Cariboo area. As the first editors of the journal noted, it is "written from day to day under all kinds of conditions ... [and] does not bother with style nor composition. But crammed with incidental details, it is a mine of interesting observations, accurate descriptions and vivid pen-pictures, interspersed with a rich vein of humour, simplicity and sportsmanship. It is a book that no lover of the West can ignore."

The spelling and punctuation of the sources have been retained except in cases where clarification is required, and editorial notes are included in brackets. The language reflects the prevailing attitudes of the times—the 1860s and early 20th century—and some passages would now be considered derogatory and even racist. The sources have been left in their original form in order to preserve the accuracy and historical flavour of the accounts. No disrespect is intended.

Prologue

Fraser River Gold Mines,
April 29, 1858

Friend Plimmer:

We have arrived in these mines at last, after one of the hardest trips on record. I shall not attempt to give you a narrative of the difficulties and dangers of travelling on this river, as it would be impossible for me to do justice to it at present. It was next to impossible to get up when we came, and when the river rises to its full height no canoe or boat can possibly get up or down.

*   We are now located thirty miles above the junction of the*

Prologue

Fraser and Thompson rivers, on Fraser River. The distances up are as follows: From the mouth of Fraser River to Fort Langley, thirty miles; from there to Fort Hope, sixty miles; from Fort Hope to Fort Yale, one day's travel; from Fort Yale to the Forks, eight days' travel, and from the Forks to where we are now, thirty miles; making in all about two hundred miles. About one-fourth of the canoes that attempt to come up are lost in the rapids, which extend from Fort Yale nearly to the Forks. A few days ago six men were drowned by their canoe being upset in attempting to go down. There is more danger in going down than in coming up. There can be no doubt about this country being immensely rich in gold. Almost every bar on the river from Fort Yale up will pay from $3 to $7 a day to the man, at the present stage of the water, and when the river gets low, which will be about next August, they will pay very well. One hundred and ninety-six dollars was taken out by one man last winter in a few hours, but the water was then at its lowest stage. The gold in the bars is all very fine and hard to save in a rocker, but with quicksilver properly managed, good wages can be made almost anywhere on the river as long as the bars are not actually covered with water. We have not been able to find a place yet where we can work anything but rockers; if we could get a sluice to work here we could make from $12 to $16 a day each. We only commenced work yesterday, and we are satisfied when we get fully under way we can make from $5 to $7 per day each. The prospect is better as we go up the river on the bars. The gold is not any coarser, but there is more of it. There are men at work here who have been thirty miles higher up and who say they made from $10 to $16 a day and that it can be made on high bars where the water will not trouble them until it obtains its highest point. There is also in that region diggings of coarser gold on small streams that empty into the main river; a few men have been there and proved the existence of rich diggings by bringing specimens back with them. The Indians all along the river from Fort Hope have a considerable quantity of gold in their possession that they say they dug themselves, but those above us will not point out the place where they get it, nor allow small parties of men to go up to look after it. I have seen pieces in their possession that weighed two pounds. The Indians on the river as far up as where we are have been very friendly, and I presume they will remain so, but those above us are disposed to be troublesome. We have been twenty miles above here on a bar which was paying $15 a day, but the Indians went into camp about a mile above us and forcibly took the provisions and arms from a party of four men and cut two of the party severely with their knives in the row. They came into our camp the same day and insisted that we should trade with them or leave their country. All the white men that were settled along the river in that section collected together, and, as the bar there was not large enough for us all to work on, all hands moved down here. This bar is large enough for a hundred men to work on all summer; there are now about forty men on it.

We design at present to remain here until we can get one hundred men together, when we will move up above the Falls and do just about what we please without regard to the Indians. There can be no doubt about the existence of rich mines of coarse gold in many parts of this country, but there have not been men enough here yet to even prospect it. We are at present the highest up of any party of white men on the river, and we must go higher to be satisfied. Five or six dollar diggings won't do while there is better in the country. I don't apprehend any danger from the Indians at present, but there will be hell to pay after a while.

We are determined to remain here, if possible, until the river falls, when good diggings can be found anywhere. I would not advise anybody to come here until about the last of July, when I think they can get up the river without much difficulty. There is a pack trail from Fort Hope, but it cannot be travelled until the snow is off the mountains.

The prices of provisions here are as follows: flour, $35 per cwt. [hundredweight or centum weight]; *pork, $1 per lb.; beans, 50 cents per lb.; and other things in proportion. Every party that starts from the Sound should have their own supplies to last them three or four months, and should bring the largest sized Chinook canoes, as small ones are liable to swamp in the rapids. Each canoe should be provided with about thirty fathoms of strong line for towing over swift water, and every man well armed. The Indians here can beat anything alive stealing, and if they continue to improve in* *that art, they will soon be able to steal a man's food after he has eaten it. We have lost nothing so far but a little sugar, but others have suffered severely. We are all in good health and spirits and expect to make a raise here before we leave. We have all promised to write to different persons in Seattle, but this will have to do for all at present.*

Yours truly,
Franklin Matthias

1

Stampede to
Fraser River Gold

WHO DISCOVERED PLACER GOLD IN British Columbia? And when? And where? Perhaps no questions concerning our past have been so much debated.

Chief Trader [*Donald*] McLean at Kamloops is alleged to have procured gold dust from the natives as early as 1852. This is supported by Gavin Hamilton, a Chief Factor of the Hudson's Bay Company [*HBC*], but in reference to a later year. He says it "is absolutely certain that gold was discovered in the Thompson River during the season of 1856, because Mr. McLean at Kamloops had two pint pickle bottles half full of gold taken from the river that year."

Roderick Finlayson [*an HBC chief factor who in 1843 assisted in founding Fort Victoria*] claimed that gold was discovered on the Thompson River and that Chief Trader McLean sent to Victoria for iron spoons to be used in extracting the nuggets from the crevices of the bedrock. James Houston of Langley claimed to be the discoverer of gold in British Columbia. His story was that in 1854 he came from the Columbia River by way of Okanagan, and stopped at the Hudson's Bay Company's old post at Tranquille Creek, near Kamloops. In the following month, to the astonishment of all the men there, he found coarse gold near the point where the Tranquille empties into the Thompson. This gold he sent to Governor Douglas, and it was, according to Mr. Houston, the first intimation that officer had of the existence of placer gold on the Mainland.

Wherever gold was first found in British Columbia, there is little doubt that the discovery which brought the Fraser region into notice, and hence is claimed by many as the original discovery, was made on the Nicomen River, which flows into the Thompson a few miles east of Lytton. Governor Douglas in his diary says: "Gold was first found on Thompson River by an Indian a quarter of a mile below Nicomen. He is since dead. The Indian was taking a drink out of the river; having no vessel he was quaffing from the stream when he perceived a shining pebble which he picked up, and it proved to be gold. The whole tribe forthwith began to collect the glittering metal. This was likely in 1856."

American adventurers began to resort to the country with the first news of gold discoveries. In 1857 they made their way from the Columbia into the watershed of the Thompson River. The natives, having learned the value of the yellow metal, threatened to prevent all attempts at mining on any of the tributaries of the Thompson. The miners, nevertheless, entered that territory, prospected the streams, and found gold. The great area covered by them in these researches gave ground for a well-founded opinion that the whole territory was gold bearing. In December 1857, Governor Douglas reported: "The reputed wealth of the Couteau mines [*the local name for the Thompson–Fraser River area*] is causing much excitement amongst the population of the United States of Washington and Oregon, and I have no doubt that a great number of people from those territories will be attracted thither in spring."

[*The governor's prediction quickly became fact, triggered by the action of the Hudson's Bay Company. By now the Natives had mined about 800 ounces (22,680 grams) of gold and traded it to the HBC. Since the gold was no use in its raw state, and the nearest mint was in San Francisco, the HBC shipped it south on the steamship* Otter *in February 1858. The news quickly spread, and in March a vanguard of prospectors arrived on the Fraser River. A few miles above Fort Hope, they discovered rich pay on a bar they named Hill's, after the man who washed the first gold. News of their success and samples of the gold were back in San Francisco by April, and the rush started to the Fraser River.*]

Fortune beckoned to the downhearted of Oregon and

California, and pointed towards the yellow star now rising above the unknown wild of New Caledonia [central BC]. The lure of the gold is always strong; in these circumstances it was irresistible. The excitement increased daily. As Donald Fraser, the Times correspondent, wrote: "None too poor and none too rich to go. None too young and none too old to go; even the decrepit go." Rumour painted the Couteau country as a second California or Australia in point of mineral wealth.

From the Territory of Washington, boats, canoes, and every species of small craft poured their human cargoes into the Fraser River District. On Puget Sound shipping was paralyzed. All the crews deserted and rushed en masse to make their fortunes in the mines. All manufacturing, all industry was at a standstill. No ties were strong enough to resist the golden influences. Even the soldiers in United States posts of Steilacoom, Forts Townsend and Bellingham deserted in numbers. But in California the excitement was, if possible, even more intense. On April 25th, the *Commodore* arrived from San Francisco with 450 miners. Governor Douglas reported on May 8th that "Not less than one thousand whites are already at work and on the way to the gold districts." A week later he increased his estimate, stating that "fifteen hundred white miners, at the smallest computation, had reached the diggings." All through the month of May vessels of every size and kind sailed from San Francisco laden with eager treasure seekers.

[During April, May, June and July, 16,144 people left

San Francisco for the Fraser River, most landing at Fort Victoria. The greatest crowd leaving San Francisco on any one day was 1,723 on July 3; July 10 saw 1,409 embark.]

The enumeration given only relates to the emigration through San Francisco. It may be added that these official figures are much smaller than the numbers which common report stated were being carried by the various vessels. For comparison, the following are given: On July 1st, the *Sierra Nevada* landed 1,900; on July 8th, the *Orizaba* and the *Cortez* together brought 2,800. [*The latter had officially taken on board only 1,300 passengers.*] We may safely conclude that every vessel was carrying, without regard to coasting laws or safety, all who wished to embark. How nearly the reported numbers approached the actual numbers can only be surmised. With the necessary allowance in this respect and with the addition of those who came from Oregon and Washington, from St. Paul, from Salt Lake City, and other western points, from the Hawaiian Islands and the various ports of Central and Southern America, it is perhaps fair to say that at least 25,000 persons were borne on that tide.

The scene in California is thus described: "The roads from the mountains were lined with foot-passengers on their way to San Francisco. Stage coaches came rolling into Sacramento, groaning under their living cargo of sturdy miners. The worm-eaten wharves of San Francisco trembled almost daily under the tread of the vast multitudes that gathered to see a northern steamer leave. With that reckless disregard of human life so characteristic of the American ship-owner, old hulks, which had long been known to be unseaworthy and rotten, were refitted for the new El Dorado. Engines, rusty from years of idleness, were polished up; leaky boilers were repatched—paint and putty filling gaping seams; and with names often changed to hide their former reputations, steamer after steamer sailed from our port, loaded to the guards with freight, and black with the crowds who were rushing to the newly-discovered land of gold."

As the Reverend R.C. Lundin Brown says, "In short, never in the history of the migrations of men has been seen such a 'rush,' so sudden and so fast."

The newspapers eagerly sought for and published every scrap of information about the mines. The excited public avidly devoured every item. In April, the *Pioneer and Democrat*, a newspaper published in Olympia, Washington, stated that within a few months the Hudson's Bay Company had traded with the Indians 110 pounds of coarse gold procured from surface workings with crude implements. The same issue stated that between 150 and 200 miners were already at work on the Fraser, and that 3 men had obtained $800 as the result of 10 days' work.

The early arrivals were not slow in sending out glowing accounts of the prospects. These were read even more greedily than the newspapers. The following are reproduced as samples [*See also the letter from Franklin Matthias in the Prologue*]:

Hell's Gate rapids and other rapids along the Fraser River drowned scores of miners. ROYAL BC MUSEUM, BC ARCHIVES C-0429

To R.R. Rees, Portland, Oregon
May 28, 1858

I am now on Fraser River, not far from Fort Yale, and am mining; and I suppose you have heard various reports from these mines. As far as I know, they are as good as I have ever seen. The river is very high now and rising fast, and we have to work on the highest bars, yet make from $12 to $50 to each rocker, so you may know what we can do when the river falls. We have sluices, also, although the gold is very fine and we lose much of it without quicksilver. Now, if you want to come here, I will say this—that this is the best mining region that I have ever yet seen; and I want you to tell Wm. Bridge to come with goods if he wants to come, for everything commands a high price here, etc. Be sure and write to him and tell him to start by the first of July, or any time, as I presume he can come where we are at any time; and if he has anything for sale he can sell it here at almost his own terms; and tell all my friends in Portland the contents of this letter, etc. Tell them that we are now working entirely on the river bars, and go down from two inches to two feet and make $8 to $50—or I may say from $6 to $50; and if you come and don't find it as I say, I am here—take any revenge; but don't let any other reports prevent you if you start.

Come if you come at all, to Olympia; there purchase a good canoe, and get you some Indians and come right along, and you will find us eight miles from Fort Yale.

S. Allen

Each incoming vessel spoke of hundreds of adventurers chafing restlessly in San Francisco, anxiously awaiting an opportunity to obtain passage to the new gold fields. Lieutenant Mayne [*Richard Mayne, a British naval officer at Esquimalt near Fort Victoria in what was then the Colony of Vancouver Island*], speaking of this period, says: "That road, too, from Esquimalt to Victoria, about which so much has since been said, in and out of the Colonial Assembly, was changed with the rest almost beyond recognition. Only a few months before, we used to flounder through the mud without meeting a single soul; now it was covered with pedestrians toiling along, with the step and air of men whose minds are occupied with thoughts of business; crowded with well-laden carts and vans, with Wells Fargo's or Freeman's 'Expresses' and with strangers of every tongue and country, in every variety of attire. Day after day on they came to Victoria, on their way to the Fraser, the greater part of them with no property but the bundle they carried, and with 'dollars, dollars, dollars!' stamped on every face."

The majority of those who sailed from San Francisco debarked at Victoria, though some went on to ports on Puget Sound. Wherever they landed about two hundred miles lay between them and the mining region. The greatest of their difficulties were before them. There were no regular means of communication with the Fraser River, and they were compelled for the first two or three months to make their way as best they could, either by boats or canoes or some kind of sailing vessel, to its mouth. The treacherous waters of the Strait of Georgia took their toll. Many were never heard of after leaving Victoria. But nothing daunted them. They battled the fierce tide-rips and the sudden gales with grim determination. Even after they entered the river, troubles and dangers were their lot. The freshet-swollen stream opposed their advance.

Speaking on this subject, in May, Governor Douglas said: "Many accidents have happened in the dangerous rapids of that river; a great number of canoes having been dashed to pieces and their cargoes swept away by the impetuous stream, while of the ill-fated adventurers who accompanied them, many have been swept into eternity." Yet during the first week of June fifty canoes, containing an average of six persons, reached Fort Hope in safety.

2

Northward up
the Fraser River

EARLY IN AUGUST [1858] DIFFICULTIES with the Indians
forced the miners above Yale to flee in terror to that place.
Those who saved their lives were robbed of tools and provisions—a serious loss, indeed, at that time. Many were unable
to make their escape, and their bodies, in some instances
scalped, came floating down the raging river. The cause of
the trouble was a combination of influences: the desire of
the Indians to monopolize the mining, the successes of the
Indians in the war in Washington then in progress, the arro-
gance of the miners, especially the American miners, who
acted as though the Indian had no rights, and, lastly, the inter-
ference with the Indian women. The natives were reported to
be obtaining firearms and firewater from the Chinese.

A rifle company of forty was organized by Captain Rouse and set out with packs on their backs on August 9th to force a passage to the Forks [*Lytton*]. The details of the movements of this company are variously reported, but it appears that, reaching the Rancheria [*Spuzzum*], they engaged in a contest with the Indians in which some seven of the latter were killed; continuing in their work of destruction they burned three Indian villages and attacked the natives wherever they met them.

The storm centre was the Big Canyon [*Hell's Gate*]. There a large body of savages congregated, taking possession of the points of vantage with the intention of barring the further advance of the whites. The trouble could scarcely have occurred at a more opportune time. The population of Yale, including the refugees, was in excess of three thousand, all waiting like owners of tickets in some great lottery for the drawing to commence. A meeting of nearly two thousand was held. A call for volunteers was issued, and [*many*] responded.

Opinions were divided as to the course to be pursued. Forty of the volunteers selected [*Captain*] Graham as their commander, and determined to follow a policy of extermination; but the remainder, believing in conciliation and sufficient exhibition of force to obtain this end, placed themselves under H.M. Snyder as captain. In the fort was a case of rifles; at first Mr. Allard, the [*Hudson's Bay*] company's officer in charge, refused to supply these weapons, but as matters now assumed a more threatening attitude, the miners demanded and obtained them. Captain Snyder induced the "war-to-the-knife" faction to lag behind to enable him to settle matters.

Leaving Yale on August 18th with one hundred and twenty-three volunteers and provisions for five days, Captain Snyder made his course up the river. At Spuzzum reinforcements joined his party. At China Bar the party were surprised to find some five miners in a sort of a fortification. Amongst these persons was Edward Stout, one of the earliest of the pioneer miners. This party, which had originally consisted of twenty-five miners, had been well to the forefront in the ascent of the river, had then advanced through the canyons to Lytton, and thence up the Thompson, prospecting and mining as they went. Warned of the hostile intentions of the natives, they had stealthily made their way down the river, avoiding the usual lines of travel, but, in spite of the utmost precautions, their movements were discovered and they were harassed by a running fire. Man by man was picked off by bullet or Indian arrow until but five were left, and of these scarcely one but bore wounds more or less severe.

The display of force had its effect. Treaties of peace and amity were concluded with all the chiefs between Yale and Lytton, including Spintlum, a noted Thompson River chief. The expedition under Snyder returned on August 25, accompanied by five of the chiefs, having established peace on

Edward Stout was among 25 miners attacked by Natives in the Fraser Canyon in 1858; only 5 survived. Stout was hit by seven arrows but recovered. He was one of the group who discovered Williams Creek, the richest of all the streams. Stout died at Yale in 1924, aged 99, and is commemorated by Stout's Gulch at Barkerville.

that portion of the river. Only two men were lost on the undertaking—Captain Graham and his lieutenant, the leaders of the extermination section, who were shot by Indians at Long Bar for having trampled down a flag of truce. With news of the satisfactory adjustment of the trouble, the miners streamed out of Yale to reoccupy their ground and be ready to take advantage of the expected fall of the waters.

In August the long looked for fall of the river commenced; between the 5th and the 12th it fell four feet and a half at Yale. But hope was doomed to disappointment. Again the waters rose, and a further period of enforced delay occurred. The river was struggling desperately to retain its wealth. About the end of August the real fall began. In a few days 200 men were at work on Fort Yale Bar, and 400 on Hill's Bar.

Like peaks above the deluge, the bars began to appear with the gradual recession and were greedily seized upon by the waiting hundreds. Miners were now scattered all along the river from Fort Langley to Pavilion Creek, the northerly boundary of the Couteau country, a distance of about 200 miles. The mining was still almost entirely bar mining. These bars were merely the exposed river bottom— sandy flats occurring in the river bends. For ages the Fraser, rushing madly along, had torn away the gold-bearing rock, crushed it in its natural setting and deposited the gold with its accompanying metallic sand in the eddies in these bends.

With the recession of the water these bars became the scenes of great activity. Although in the painful interval of waiting—June to September—thousands had left the country and, notwithstanding that the size of a claim was but twenty-five feet square, the bars below the canyon were overcrowded. There was no bedrock in these sands, but there was, nevertheless, a recognized pay stratum, clearly defined and differing in color from the worthless sand of the bar. This auriferous deposit was sometimes situated a few inches below the surface, at other places it was two feet or even more. It also varied in thickness.

On Hill's Bar, it was claimed to have been six feet thick and sixty feet wide, extending the whole length of the bar, a distance of fully half a mile, and yielding on the average 50 cents a pan. As an instance of the richness of this bar, it is recorded that Mr. Winston and two partners took out forty-six pounds of gold dust between December 1858, and April 1859. Frequently they obtained fifty ounces in a day and sometimes, when the sluices were running day and night, seventy to eighty ounces in the same time.

In September, Alfred Waddington counted 800 rockers at work between Fort Hope and Fort Yale. In November, Douglas reported that there were over 10,000 persons engaged in mining, of whom one-half were between Murderer's Bar [*located just below Hope*] and Fort Yale. This did not, by any means, indicate that the bars in that locality were the richest; but that access to the diggings above the canyons was so difficult, the supply of food so precarious, and its price so high that all but the most resolute and adventurous were deterred.

It is impossible to enter into the details of the output of the various bars. The total for the six months—June to December, 1858—was $520,353. Hill's Bar was admitted on all sides to be the richest, and, besides being the first discovered in the advance of 1858, was the longest mined. The other bars, it may be said in a general way, varied in productiveness from those which barely paid meagre wages to those that produced three and four ounces per man per day.

These bars formed but stepping-stones for the restless, roaming miners, who pressed on and on up the river, finding gold wherever they prospected, but never satisfied, striving ever to discover those richer diggings, the existence of which was heresy to deny. [Fort] Alexandria was reached, and then the bars above that place were tested and rich diggings were found in that vicinity. Still "onward" was the cry. By the month of May, the Quesnel River [about 400 miles upstream] had been reached. Rumors of great "strikes" there were current. But the Lure of the Gold was strong; it drew the seekers on. The Fraser was examined and prospected for a distance of one hundred and fifty miles beyond Fort George [today's Prince George]. Every bar was reported as promising from $5 to $6 per day to the man. Better fortune came to those who left the Fraser and ascended the Quesnel.

Northward up the Fraser River

Late in 1859, after prospecting its bars, which proved far richer than those of the main river, Cariboo Lake was found. In cumbersome rafts, bound together with withes [*willow shoots*], they made their way along its shores. Now their perseverance was rewarded. Rich strikes, in some cases $200 per day per man, were reported. Gold in large quantities was also found on the Horsefly River, which flows into Quesnel Lake from the southward. There a party of five men in one week, with two rockers, took out one hundred and one ounces. One of the foremost in the advance into the Horsefly was Dud Moreland, who later settled at Cottonwood.

Over and above these material results, which showed a large area to be auriferous, and some sections to be especially so, the season of 1859 was eminently satisfactory. In the territory around Quesnel and Cariboo Lakes, the California miners found an indication which gladdened their hearts—the "Blue Lead" as it was called, which in California was the gold-bearing stratum. It was traced for thirty miles with a lateral extent of nearly ten miles. It is a question, much debated, whether the real California blue lead existed in British Columbia; but that is beside the point, for the miners believed it did and acted on that assumption. Shafts were sunk to a depth of twenty-five feet to reach the bed-rock, with its covering of blue clay, the alleged blue lead. The results were satisfactory, though the season was too far advanced for any comprehensive attempts.

[*During 1860, about 4,000 miners were panning and*

rocking the gravel of creeks and rivers throughout BC, with some 3,000 of them on the Fraser River and its tributaries north of Lillooet. Most found gold, but to those who ventured up the Quesnel River fell the ultimate bonanza. In the fall of 1860, "Doc" Keithley, George Weaver and their companions came across a creek that flowed into Cariboo Lake from a northerly direction. They named it Keithley after its discoverer and headed into the thick underbrush to test its gravel.]

It was the first of the real Cariboo creeks and soon became one of the most famous, though not at all a rich creek, as compared with its more famous neighbors. The creek itself, as well as its tributary, Snowshoe, and Harvey and Cunningham Creeks, which flow from the eastward face of Bald Mountain, had been discovered early in 1860. But the absence of gold-bearing stratum on the surface had delayed its exploitation, and it was not until late in the fall of that year that its auriferous character was ascertained. It rose at once into prominence as a supply centre for the entire region of the North Quesnel River. The creeks which radiate from Bald Mountain: Keithley, Harvey, Cunningham, Snowshoe, Grouse, Antler, Lowhee, Williams, and Lightning appear to occupy the same location, but not the identical channel of gold-bearing creeks. Where gold was first found on them is said to have been the spot where erosion had laid bare, or nearly bare, for short distances, the deeper channels of the ancient streams.

At the 6,000-foot level of the Cariboo Mountains, snow lingers until July or later and can return by September. The peaks in this photograph are part of the Snowshoe Plateau, headwaters of Antler, Williams, Cunningham, Keithley and other creeks whose gravel yielded gold by the ton. HERITAGE HOUSE

Late in the fall of 1860, John Rose [*who met a tragic death in 1863*] and his partner McDonald, with "Doc" Keithley and George Weaver, set out from Keithley Creek in search of new diggings. Ascending that creek for about five miles, they took a course northeastward up a ravine. Reaching Snowshoe Creek, a branch of Keithley, they followed it to its source, some six or seven miles further, near the summit of the watershed dividing the streams flowing into Cariboo Lake from those flowing eastward, northward, and westward into Bear, Willow, and Cottonwood Rivers. Thence the whole surrounding country lay unrolled before them.

Northward and eastward the horizon was bounded by rugged and lofty mountains; towards the west and north-west the prospect was more level; while immediately below lay rolling hills intersected by valleys and ravines! 'Twas man's first view of Cariboo. Over the whole region lay the mantle of solitude and silence—gold existing without contention or struggle. Traversing this summit in the same general direction they came upon another creek, at a distance of about twenty miles from Keithley. The creek [*Antler*] winds through the centre of a narrow valley and is surmounted by hills sloping down to flats and benches of alluvial deposit. The bed-rock on which gold was found lay but a short distance under the surface, and in many places cropped out. Here was the richest deposit yet found in British Columbia—considerable quantities of gold being found on the bare rock.

One pan produced $25, a second, $75. The fortunate prospectors, however, had their ardour somewhat cooled the next morning by awakening to find a foot of snow on the ground. Here, again, besides the actual value of the find, was the strengthening of their faith in the auriferous nature of the country. They found a kind of slate rock covered with red gravel and said to bear a close resemblance to the gold-producing beds of Californian streams. These discoverers tried to keep the secret; but gold, like murder, will out.

Returning to Keithley Creek for provisions, an incautious word at "Red-headed" Davis's store gave the clue. In mid-winter, on snowshoes, over four or five feet of snow, miners set out from Keithley to stake the vacant ground on Antler. Many claims were recorded, and, in several instances, the same ground was taken up by different parties. This led to disputes. Mr. Nind, the Gold Commissioner for the district with headquarters at William's Lake, came in over the snow to settle these conflicting claims. Arriving in March 1861, he found, on Antler Creek, one log cabin built by Rose and McDonald. The remainder of the men were living in holes dug in the snow, which was six or seven feet deep. Even under these conditions some prospecting was being carried on, with successful results, though the labor of clearing away the snow and sinking holes to bed-rock was excessive.

CHAPTER

3

The Golden Creeks
of Cariboo

BUT ANTLER CREEK WAS ONLY the portal of Cariboo, a region studded with mountains of considerable altitude, closely packed together. This creek coursed around the greatest of the three great peaks of Cariboo—Mount Agnes, commonly called Bald Mountain. Impressively grand and sublime are these majestic spurs of the Rockies towering to six and seven thousand feet. The land of Golden Promise, so firmly believed in, so earnestly sought for, lay just on the other side of Mount Agnes, only twelve miles away.

When the mid-winter rush was made upon Antler Creek, a party, amongst whom were Edward Stout, Michael Burns, "Fidele" or Vital, and William Dietz (commonly called Dutch Bill), started in search of other fields. Crossing the ridge which culminates in Mount Agnes, they kept to the northward and descended upon a creek which forms the headwaters of Willow River. This was Williams Creek, the richest, the most celebrated of all the Cariboo creeks. Dutch Bill, its discoverer, after whom it was named, found gold at the canyon about halfway between Richfield and Barkerville, as afterwards located.

At first Williams Creek gave no hint of its immense deep-hidden wealth. The canyon where discovery was made was the very poorest part. Dutch Bill's prospecting gave about 75 cents to the pan, yet that was good pay, but in no way suggestive, even to the optimistic, of the world-renowned richness of the Steele, the Diller, the Cameron, and the Ericson claims. Returning, the party spread the news of their find, and pell mell went the mad rush to Williams Creek. No roads or trails existed in the Cariboo country at the time, and each party took the course which they judged best, for, as already mentioned, from the tops of the ridges Cariboo was like an open book.

Thus in making from Quesnel River and Keithley Creek to Williams, the miners came upon Lightning Creek, which empties into Swift River, and Lowhee Creek, flowing into Jack of Clubs Lake. The origins of these names may be of interest. The latter creek was discovered by Richard Willoughby in 1861 and named by him in honor of the "Great Lowhee," a secret society at Yale, in which he was a prominent member. The former owes its name to the following

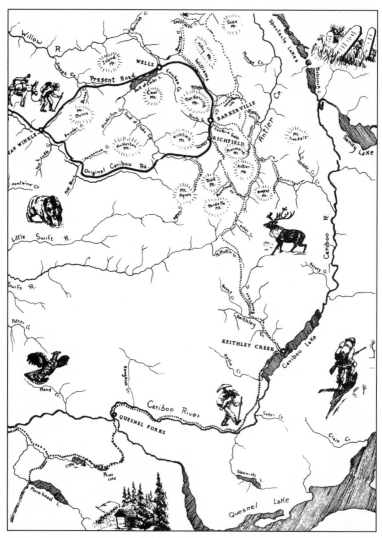

This map shows the creeks of Cariboo, the present road to Barkerville and the original wagon road from Van Winkle. The first route to the gold-rich region was up the Cariboo River to Keithley Creek, then northward to Snowshoe Creek and the 6,000-foot level of the Cariboo Mountains. GWEN LEWIS incident. A party, while traveling through its valley, were suddenly overtaken by one of those thunderstorms common in the mountain regions. One of the party, feeling greatly inconvenienced by the severity of the storm—being drenched to the skin—exclaimed aloud, "Boys, this is lightning," feeling fully convinced that this was the most emphatic expression he could use to express his opinion of the inclement weather.

Another version of this story is that "Early in 1861, Bill Cunningham, Jack Hume, and Jim Bell, three gold hunters, started southward over the mountains from Jack of Clubs Creek on a prospecting tour. They found the trip exceedingly rough and laborious, especially in descending the steep banks of the creek they came to. The former called out to his companions, 'Boys, this is lightning,' it being a favourite expression with him in meeting anything difficult to overcome."

Every creek proved to be gold-bearing. The news of their richness lost nothing by repetition and the Fraser, Thompson, and the Rock Creek diggings, which for some time had been gradually falling into the hands of the Chinese, were practically abandoned to them. So the spring and summer of 1861 saw the mountains of Cariboo swarming with eager miners, many of whom had left good diggings in the lower country.

Williams Creek, for a time, gave such poor results that it was called Humbug Creek. During the early summer of

1861 mining was confined to the portion above the canyon. There the pay dirt, the bed of the old creek, lay close to the surface, usually within eight or twelve feet. At that depth, a hard blue clay was met which was supposed to be the bedrock, and upon it good pay was found. But later in that year Mr. Abbott of the Jourdan and Abbott claim, while his partner was away for the day obtaining provisions, concluded to go through this clay and ascertain what lay below. Piercing it, he found below a stratum of gold-bearing gravel, so rich that when his partner returned, after a lapse of forty-eight hours, he produced fifty ounces as the result of his explorations. Up to this time only six claims on the creek had produced gold. With this news all was changed. Hundreds crowded other hundreds in a mad rush.

The whole creek and the hillside for a distance of six miles was literally covered with miners and mining claims, now increased to 100 feet square. The only spot neglected, strange as it may seem, was the spot in the canyon where Dutch Bill had first found gold. But while above the canyon the diggings were shallow, permitting the barren covering to be washed off and the use of sluices and bed-rock flumes, yet below the canyon conditions were totally different. The pay dirt there lay fifty or sixty feet below the present level. Shafts must be sunk, drifts made, and tunnels driven. Pumps would be required to keep the workings dry, and hoisting gear to raise the dirt to the surface to be washed. This work could be carried on throughout the year, while the advent of winter prevented all operations in the surface diggings above the canyon.

Governor Douglas reported that the least Abbott and Jourdan took out, with three men, was one hundred and twenty ounces per day. Judge Begbie reported in September 1861 that the Abbott and Jourdan claim and the Steele claim, which were both in the shallow diggings above the canyon, were producing thirty to forty pounds of gold per day, and that Steele had informed him that they had taken out in one day three hundred and seventy ounces. The greatest day's yield of the Steele claim in 1861 was four hundred and nine ounces.

On Lowhee, Willoughby, the discoverer, with from four to seven men, between July 27 and September 8, 1861, took out three thousand and thirty-seven ounces, worth $50,000 [*gold was then about $16 an ounce*], from a strip four hundred feet along the creek by twelve feet wide. In no place did his excavation to bed-rock exceed four feet, and usually but three. A Mr. Patterson and his brother brought back $10,000 as a result of five weeks' mining on Lowhee. Their largest day's return was seventy-three ounces, worth about $1,200. The gold on this creek was in rough, jagged pieces, sometimes weighing six or even ten ounces.

On Lightning Creek, Mr. Ball reported on October 1, 1861, that one Ned Campbell had taken out the almost fabulous sums of nine hundred ounces the first day, five hundred ounces the second day, and three hundred ounces the third day. Another authority says that this claim, which cost $25,000 to open, returned $100,000 in three months.

The returns from Antler Creek for 1861, while respectable, are far below such colossal figures as the above. One company of four men were making from four ounces to nine and one-fourth ounces each per day; and the ordinary yield was from $20 to $50 per day for each man employed. The Reverend R.C. Lundin Brown records his being present when $1,000 were taken out of the sluice boxes as the result of one day's work.

On Keithley Creek, in 1861, the returns were smaller. Several companies were making from $50 to $100 per day to the man in the bed of the creek, and somewhat better in the bench diggings. Most of the miners were making from two ounces to three ounces per day. During this summer there were some two hundred men on the creek. Outside of the mining upon the creek itself, Keithley—the collection of houses at the mouth of the creek—was the supply centre for the Cariboo Lake and North Quesnel region.

So ends the year 1861. Taken all in all, a very successful year. Statistics give the output of gold for 1861 as $2,666,118. But behind this, and more important, was the general feeling that all the creeks of Cariboo were gold-bearing. To the outside world went reports of great "finds"—stories of men who in a season sprung from penury to wealth—exaggerated tales of rich deposits as wondrous as those that Ali Baba and Aladdin found.

Said the Puget Sound Herald: "The excitement respecting the Cariboo mines is fast reaching fever heat in this vicinity. People will not think of or talk about anything else, even the battles of the Rebellion are forgotten or cease to interest them, so engrossing is the subject of the new mines. Everybody talks of going to the Cariboo Diggings in the spring. We may, therefore, confidently look for a rush to these mines next season, equalled only by the Fraser River excitement of '58. So far as we can learn every miner from this new gold field has brought with him from $5,000 to $20,000, all of which has been obtained in the short space of two or three months."

Here was the genesis of the "rush" of 1862—not from California alone, but from the Eastern States and the Canadas [*essentially, today's Ontario, Quebec and the Maritimes*], from the British Isles and the Continent. These immigrants came principally by the recognized route by way of Panama, San Francisco, Victoria, and thence up the Fraser. But as in 1858, so in 1862; when the end of navigation was reached, miles of forbidding and dangerous land travel intervened. As the song ran:

Five hundred miles to travel where naught but mosses grew
To cheer the weary traveller on the road to Cariboo.

The Gold Commissioner of Cariboo, in the fall of 1861, had "laid over" the claims until June 1, 1862; that is to say, he had suspended until that date the operation of the law which rendered a claim invalid if it remained unworked for seventy-two hours. This was necessary, as the mining then being confined to shallow diggings—from three to twelve feet in depth—it was impossible to carry it on during the rigorous winter of Cariboo. By the end of May probably six thousand miners had entered Cariboo, making their way under great difficulties, so as to be on the ground when the "lay over" should expire. Some had in three weeks walked the whole distance from Lillooet, carrying fifty- and sixty-pound packs. Over two thousand expectant men were on Williams Creek alone.

Thus was created an unprecedented demand for food and supplies, and these, becoming very scarce, commanded famine prices. For example, flour, bacon, beans, and salt were $1.50 a pound, dried apples $2.50 a pound, and gumboots $42.50 a pair. The "lay over" period was extended to July 1st. This, with the high prices, disheartened many, who returned to the lower country. While some of the disappointed denounced the country as a humbug, the majority had faith in Cariboo, only complaining of being starved out. They were loud in their demand for a road to the mines so as to provide sufficient supplies at reasonable prices, declaring that wagons must be employed, as there were not enough mules in the colony to bring in over the miserable trails then existing the necessary food and implements.

On Williams Creek mining went on above the canyon,

where the shallow diggings continued to pay well. Edward Stout had ventured to try the mouth of Stout's Gulch, which is below the canyon, and had there found, at comparatively shallow depth, the dark colored, water-worn gold of Williams Creek. Going deeper he found the bright, jagged, and more valuable Stout's Gulch gold. Encouraged by these results, William Barker, commonly called Billy Barker, had taken up a claim still further down Williams Creek, in the vicinity of the present town of Barkerville.

The other miners ridiculed this action, believing that all the gold was above the canyon; but he persevered and drew the prize of 1862. "Billy Barker has struck the lead on Williams Creek on the flat below the canyon at a depth of fifty-two feet, obtaining $5 to the pan." A few days later the Canadian company was similarly fortunate. Then John A. Cameron, "Cariboo Cameron," found the lead even lower down the creek. Opinions changed. Below the canyon became the favorite spot. These deep diggings, from fifty to eighty feet, gave an air of permanency to Williams Creek, which contributed a large proportion of the $2,656,903 credited to the mines of the colony during 1862.

Lightning Creek, owing to the great expense attendant upon the opening of claims there, gave up a little of its treasure; still the greatest confidence was felt as to the ultimate result of operations thereon. Being most extensive, it was expected that, with the advent of cheaper supplies, it would contribute its full quota towards the general yield. In 1862 shafts were sunk from Eagle Creek to Davis Creek, along Lightning, but below Van Winkle they were uniformly unsuccessful, being unable to cope with the water. Antler Creek was regarded as coquettish in 1862. Although on its banks good prospects were obtained and rich hill diggings announced, still the result was disappointing. One claim, Murray's, yielded in three days eighty-five ounces to each man employed; another, Hoy's, gave seventy-two ounces as the result of six men's work for half a day; while a third, Edward's, produced over $3,000 in a week. These were the best, and their returns were much above the average.

The year 1863 was the banner year of Cariboo. Williams Creek was mined along a stretch of seven miles, and about four thousand men found employment there. The deep diggings below the canyon were in full swing. Gold was being produced on a scale which exceeded California in its palmiest days. The results were in many cases almost incredible. A few isolated, well-authenticated instances will be given, because the reports of such golden harvests went abroad and aided to draw to the colony many persons filled with hopes of similar success.

The Cameron claim yielded, during 1863, from forty to one hundred and twelve ounces to each of three shifts per day. In October, John A. Cameron, "Cariboo Cameron," its principal shareholder, brought out about $150,000, his share of its yield for three months. Viscount Milton and Dr. W.B. Cheadle [*Cariboo's first tourists; see Chapter 6*] saw a wash-up on the Raby, which filled one of the tin cases used for preserved meats, holding nearly a quart and valued at about $5,000, the result of fifteen hours' work. Amongst this were several shillings and quarter dollars, which had dropped out of the men's pockets and turned up again in the dump box. The Diller took out one hundred and two pounds Troy in a single day. The Cunningham produced, on an average, $2,000 per day during the whole season.

The following summary shows the returns from the principal claims on Williams Creek to the end of 1863: The Adams yielded $50,000 from 100 feet; the Steele, $120,000 from 80 feet; the Diller, $240,000 from 50 feet; the Cunningham, $270,000 from 500 feet; the Burns, $140,000 from 80 feet; the Canadian, $180,000 from 120 feet; the Neversweat, $100,000 from 120 feet; the Moffatt, $90,000 from 50 feet; the Tinker, $120,000 from 140 feet; the Wattie, $130,000 from 100 feet; besides the Black Jack Tunnel, Barker, Baldhead, Abbott, Grier, Wilson, Beauregard, Raby, Cameron, Prince of Wales, and numbers of others of world-wide fame. Forty claims at least paid handsomely, and from about twenty was taken out steadily, every twenty-four hours, from seventy to four hundred ounces.

Besides Williams Creek, [*claims at*] Keithley, Goose, Cunningham, Lightning, Jack of Clubs, Grouse, Chisholm, Sovereign, Fountain, Harvey, Nelson, Stevens, Showshoe, Last Chance, Anderson, California, Thistle, Sugar, Willow,

McCallum, Tababoo, and Lowhee each drew a share of attention, and miners were at work upon them all.

The narrow gulch of Lowhee Creek for a while bade fair to equal Williams Creek, as indeed its early production already mentioned had promised. When the bed-rock was reached on the Cornish claim, $4 to the pan was obtained, and for a considerable period between three hundred and four hundred ounces a day were taken from the Sage Miller claim.

On Lightning Creek, one company—the Butcher—working on a hill claim sixty feet above the bed of the stream, struck "pay" late in the fall of 1863, taking out two hundred ounces in one day. Another company was making forty ounces a day on this creek.

The practical completion of the Cariboo Road in 1863 greatly decreased the cost of living in that distant region. From the changed conditions flowed a further result. In the winter of 1862–63 Cariboo was practically a deserted land. Some eighty miners, only, remained. But in the following winter some five hundred or six hundred miners stayed on Williams Creek. In their moss-chinked, mud-roofed log-huts, with their large, cheerful fireplaces, they spent the short days and long nights developing a rude sort of social intercourse and whiling away the monotony with conversation and cards. Some even worked a great part of the time, for during the winter of 1863–64 a few of the claims—the Cameron, Raby, and Caledonia, for instance, being deep diggings—carried on operations. But the majority of miners and mine-owners preferred to take advantage of the annual "lay-over" and spend their winters in the more genial climate and more attractive surroundings of Victoria and San Francisco.

Cariboo drew to itself not only miners but all the classes that naturally congregate where money is plentiful and easily obtained. Gamblers flocked like vultures to the spot. The authorities resolutely set their faces against this evil, but the vice was too deeply rooted to be completely eradicated. It merely went under cover and continued to flourish in private. An anomalous class of females, known as the hurdy-gurdy girls, made their appearance in Cariboo. They were mostly of German extraction. They frequented the saloons and drinking places and, for a money consideration, danced with all applicants. But, at the same time, their morals were above reproach.

The pay streak, as the auriferous stratum was called, consisted, on Williams Creek, of a blue clay about six feet thick, mixed with gravel and decomposed slate. Above the canyon this stratum lay quite close to the surface, but below that spot the covering was, generally speaking, from fifty to sixty feet. The deepest shaft in this vicinity was one hundred and thirty-four feet, but even then it did not reach the bedrock. The prevailing theory was that this pay stratum was the bed of an old creek, which, carrying down the drift gold, had allowed it to settle either on the bed-rock or in the blue clay above it. The debris of centuries then covered the treasure. Great changes in the earth's surface took place. Here a slide, there a convulsion, upheaving a portion and distorting another. The present bed of a stream was thus no index to its old and gold-bearing bed.

Here was the element of chance—the reason why a claim on a hillside was rich, while one right in the present bed was barren. One miner might be making $1,000 a day, while his neighbor above or below him found his claim worthless. The former had struck the old bed, the latter not. It is evident that such a condition was one for capital and cooperation to cope with. The individual miner could not take the risk, even if he had the means, of sinking a shaft fifty or sixty feet in a country where wages and provisions were so expensive. Deep diggings were not for him. Hence the Peace River excitement, the Kootenay, and Big Bend rushes of 1864 and 1865.

The yield of 1863—the golden year of Cariboo—is officially given as $3,913,563, though Allan Francis, the representative of the United States, estimated it at about $6,000,000.

During 1864, the claims below the canyon on Williams Creek were all being worked and all paid in varying measures of success. The Wake-up-Jake, reaching bed-rock in this year, gave fifty-two ounces, equal to about $800, from one panful of dirt. The Ericson on Conklin Gulch, a branch of Williams Creek, which was opened in 1863, now produced a weekly return of one thousand, four hundred ounces. The Cameron claim continued to pay eighty to ninety ounces a day. In the fall, the Prairie Flower, earlier known by a far less euphonious name, struck the pay, taking out in one day one hundred and seventy ounces.

A short distance below the Cameron claim, near a spot called Marysville, Williams Creek widens into a flat, locally known as the meadows. An effort was made to work this ground in 1864. The great difficulty below the canyon, and especially in this section, was to cope with the flow of water. As soon as the Cariboo Road came into being, improved steam pumps replaced the picturesque wooden water wheels which drove the home-made pumps. But while these were sufficient in the deep ground near Camerontown and Barkerville, they were of little service in the meadows.

An artesian mining company which had obtained a twenty-year lease of a half mile square in this locality undertook a different style of work. Instead of the old-fashioned shafts, this company operated by means of an artesian well auger, bringing up a panful of dirt at each raise. For a short time they obtained good returns, the first day's washing giving one hundred and fifty ounces, but the scheme ended in failure. The regular style of mining was also tried on the meadows on a very extensive scale over a distance of about three miles, but without success, for want of adequate machinery and pumps.

The Tiger, Beaver, Richfield, and John Bull were among

the claims on the meadows which never reached bed-rock, "never bottomed," as the expression was. From the claims immediately adjoining and nearer Camerontown a small amount was obtained, but the water could not be overcome. The Marysville, Phelan, and Hart, which lay within a few hundred feet, yielded $250,000 and $300,000 each. But in these instances the pumps controlled the water.

The opinion was, therefore, always strong that the meadows would yield enormously if the water could be kept out of the workings. But neither in 1864 and 1865, nor in the days of the Lane and Kurtz Cariboo Mining Company in 1870 and 1873, could it be got under control. That company, which had a lease of a portion of this ground, did succeed, by sinking a shaft in rock to a depth of one hundred and twenty-five feet and drifting one hundred and forty-five feet under the meadows toward the old channel, in getting a prospect of $25. But just as the golden result appeared at hand, the water "slumgullion," as it was called, compelled a suspension. It was thought, in 1876, that a bed-rock flume from Valley Creek, two and one-half miles in length, might solve the riddle, but nothing was done, and the riches of the meadows, if they exist, defied the ingenuity of man.

Following the experiment of 1863, a considerable number of claims [were] worked through the winter of 1864. Amongst them were the Oram, Adams, Elliott, Prince of Wales, Cameron, Moffatt, New York, Grizzly, Caledonia, Cariboo, Watson, and Canadian. This activity gave stability and an air of permanent settlement to the Cariboo region. Of the one thousand, five hundred miners, about seven hundred or eight hundred spent the winter there. A word or two about the other creeks will suffice. On Cunningham Creek, in 1864, shallow diggings at eight to ten feet were struck. One company was taking out one hundred ounces a day with four men. In a short time four hundred miners had rushed to this creek, the majority of whom were making two to three ounces a day. On Lightning Creek, the Ayrshire Lass was producing from twenty-five to forty ounces a day, and five or six other claims were paying well. The Butcher claim took out $5,300 in three days and had the honour of producing the largest nugget found in Cariboo, thirty and one-sixteenth ounces. Lowhee Creek continued to produce regularly, but no striking returns were obtained.

The following statistics, taken from Harnett's Lectures, will give an idea of cost and returns from some of the principal mines on Williams Creek: The Cunningham claim, located in 1861, with four interests, cost $100,000 to work, and yielded, up to 1865, $500,000. The California, located at the same time, cost $150,000 to work and yielded during the same period $500,000. The Black Jack, located in 1862, with six interests, returned in two years $200,000, under a total outlay of $50,000 for work at $16 a day. The Tontine, located in 1861, with four interests, cost $100,000 up to 1865 for development and working and yielded $500,000. The Dietz paid good wages steadily. All these were in the shallow ground above the canyon. Below the canyon the High-Low-Jack, with five interests, paid in June 1867, $12,000 to the share. The Alturas, on Stout's gulch, located in 1864, with eight interests, paid off in five weeks during 1866 an indebtedness of $23,000. Its complete output was $275,000. The Taff Vale, on the same gulch, cost $30,000 to open, and yielded from one hundred to two hundred ounces per week, giving a grand total of $300,000.

In closing our remarks upon the golden era of Cariboo it is fitting to add a few words about the miners themselves. Reference has been already made to the death of John Rose. As this man was one of the most successful and energetic prospectors, a few details are given. The miners believed in his star and confidently expected that he could and would find diggings as rich as Antler and Williams Creeks. Thus his movements were the subject of careful investigation. In the spring of 1863 he set out from Williams Creek on a prospecting trip into the Bear River country. From that time no white man ever saw John Rose alive. His remains were never found, nor was any authentic information as to his end ever obtained. In Milton and Cheadle's Northwest Passage by Land it is stated that later in the summer there was found, hanging to a branch, a tin cup bearing the words, "Dying of starvation," thus indicating his end. But this is an error. The authors have confused the death of Rose with that of Donald Munro. That unfortunate man wandered into the same locality and was lost.

In June 1863, a miner, Sim Shiveley, while returning from a prospecting tour, stopped on Bear River, about one hundred and sixty miles from Richfield, to cook his dinner. Wandering along its bank he noticed a cloth hanging to a tree. His curiosity being aroused, he hastened to the spot and found there the gruesome remains of a man. At his head was a tin cup bearing these words: "Donald Munro, in the woods, lost June, 1863, is from Inverness Town, Scotland, born June, 1825." Not an ounce of food was found near the body. But the stripped bark of the neighboring trees spoke eloquently of his desperate efforts to sustain life. Rolling the dead man in his blankets, Shiveley buried him there.

Of all the miners of the early days in Cariboo none is more widely known than John A. Cameron. This man's spectacular rise to wealth entitled him to the sobriquet he bore—"Cariboo Cameron." Returning to Glengarry, Canada [*in today's Ontario*], in the fall of 1863, he purchased a farm of two hundred acres at Summers Town on the St. Lawrence and expended vast sums in improving it, but it proved a poor investment. He then purchased some steamboat stock and a sawmill and timber limits on Lake Superior. These, likewise, turned out badly. As a last desperate chance he staked the remainder of his money on a quartz mine in Nova Scotia. Still ill-fortune pursued him. He lost all. In 1888 he returned to Cariboo to make another fortune, in vain. He died there on November 7, 1888, aged sixty-eight years. His body, most fittingly, rests in the quiet little cemetery at Camerontown on Williams Creek, overlooking the scene of his unparalleled success.

As an example of the difficulties of transportation before the advent of the Cariboo wagon road, the following incident is reproduced. It will serve to cast a light upon the nature of the men of '62.

Early in October 1862, Mr. Moses Cross Ireland, with some others, was returning from Cariboo across Bald Mountain. They had reached within a short distance of a well-known landmark in that desolate district called the "colored man's house" when the snow fell so thickly that they could not see an object ahead of them. They lost the trail and, travelling about for some four miles, came on another party lost like themselves. Shortly afterwards they were joined by another man, Frank Fulford, a packer. He informed them that about half a mile farther on were a number of people, including Mrs. Webster and her two daughters, Mrs. Cusheon, and a girl of fourteen.

After a debate with his companions on the situation, no two agreeing, Mr. Ireland struck out in the direction where he thought the lost trail lay. Upon his taking the resolution six others decided to join him. They wandered about until night-fall without satisfaction and were preparing to camp for the night when the welcome sound of a gun report attracted their attention and they made for the place they judged it came from. Soon they were rejoicing in the colored man's cabin where they remained for the night.

Early next morning they found the snow was four feet deep, but with three others Mr. Ireland started to rescue the party lost in the snow, some thirty in number. On reaching a high point on the mountain they encountered so much snow that they were obliged to return. Rigging up some kind of snow shoes they again started on their mission of mercy and discovered the lost party about sundown.

They were camped in a ravine cowering round a fire with some blankets rigged up to break the piercing cold wind that howled through the forest. Men, women, and children, with some surviving animals, were huddled together in a wretched state, their teeth chattering and eyes swollen by the smoke driven in all directions by the icy blast. They had been fasting for sixty hours and eagerly welcomed the provisions the rescue party had brought with them. They told Mr. Ireland that Frank Fulford and another man had left them to search for provisions.

Mr. Ireland saw from the deplorable straits the people were in that considerable assistance would be necessary to get them out of their perilous position on account of the depth of the snow. Leaving his companions with them, he started out for help, hallooing as he went in case other benighted travelers might be within hearing and be attracted. One of his calls was answered from a canyon about half way back, to which he proceeded and there he found Fulford and his comrade.

They had struggled through the snow all day and at

length, overcome by hunger, fatigue and cold, had given up all hope. Mr. Ireland supplied them with some food. Invigorated with that, and the confidence imparted by the presence of their deliverer, they crawled over the snow on their hands and knees for about a mile, where they reached the summit of the ridge. Here they traveled more easily down hill to the colored man's cabin, where they arrived about 9 o'clock that night.

When Mr. Ireland reported the miserable condition of the unfortunates he had left, about twenty men volunteered to accompany him to the rescue. Next morning they began their toilsome journey as soon as they could see daylight. Breaking a trail through the deep snow, they succeeded in getting the whole party, including the surviving animals, back to that haven of rest, the colored man's cabin, in safety. Mrs. Webster was placed upon the stoutest animal and the youngest daughter was occasionally carried by Mr. Ireland.

Thus were a party of thirty persons providentially rescued, mainly through the perseverance, courage, and foresight of a heroic gentleman, Mr. Ireland. He was overwhelmed with the grateful thanks of the rescued party, who clamorously insisted upon bestowing pecuniary rewards upon their rescuer, which he as persistently declined.

4

Roads and Trails to the Goldfields

WHEN THE MINERS ARRIVED IN 1858 the only trails leading from the lower Fraser region were the abandoned trail of the Hudson's Bay Company from Fort Kamloops to Fort Yale, and the existing trail from Fort Kamloops to Fort Hope. These routes were of comparatively small value to persons wishing to ascend the Fraser. Moreover, owing to their elevation, they were snowbound about eight months of the year. But there existed then, as there had existed from the earliest times of which we have any record, Indian trails along the banks of the river—trails of which Simon Fraser has left such a vivid description.

[*The problems of 1858 were*] to get supplies into the region beyond Yale and to reach the mining bars above the

Chief Trader Alexander Caulfield Anderson of the Hudson's Bay Company discovered and mapped a route around the Fraser Canyon. ROYAL BC MUSEUM, BC ARCHIVES A-01075

canyons . . . The raging torrent closed the river; the approach must be by land. The "almost insurmountable barrier" which the country beyond Yale presented caused Governor Douglas to give his attention to a route by way of the chain of lakes from Harrison Lake to the Fraser at Lillooet. This line of communication had been long known to the Hudson's Bay Company and had been mapped by Mr. A.C. Anderson, one of their chief traders. The fact that only short bits of trail were necessary to connect the stretches of water appealed strongly to Douglas. The question he had to solve, however, was how to build these bits, short as they were, with very limited funds.

Late in July 1858, he invited the miners then in Victoria to consider the undertaking. The arrangement ultimately made was unique. Five hundred miners, divided into twenty companies of twenty-five men each under the command of a captain, were to be given free transportation from Victoria to the point where the trail was to commence, and to be supplied free food during its construction. They were to receive no remuneration for their labour in building the trail. Each miner was to deposit $25 as security for the fulfilment of his agreement, which sum was to be repaid in provisions at Victoria prices when the work was completed, together with a fair allowance to cover the carriage of such provisions to the end of the trail.

The first detachment, two hundred and fifty men, left Victoria in the *Otter* on August 5, 1858; the remainder followed on the 10th. Their first act was to name the western terminus of the trail Port Douglas, in honour of the Governor. At the outset the work progressed rapidly. Ten miles were built during the first four days, and when the whole body was at work, from four to six miles daily. But the transportation of materials and supplies became more serious with the increasing distance. It was supposed that mules would be put on the finished trail for this purpose, and thus it was expected that the work would be completed in four or five weeks. Some delay and considerable dissatisfaction arose over the failure to supply these animals promptly, for in the interval all supplies had to be carried by the men themselves.

The trail was completed about the end of September. It was not a mere mule trail, but was well built, with bridges at all necessary points, and almost sufficiently wide for wagon use. Its entire length, including the lakes, was about one hundred miles. As completed, goods could be packed over it for 20 cents a pound. Some difficulty occurred in arranging the amount to be allowed for the transportation of the road-makers' supplies from Douglas to Lillooet. The men thought that 20 cents a pound should be allowed, while the representative of the Government would allow but 4 cents. When the question came before the Governor himself, he directed that the promised supplies be either transported over the trail to Fraser River at the Colony's expense, or a fair allowance, which he fixed at 18 cents a pound, be made to the men.

This trail gave ready access to the Fraser at Lillooet, reducing, consequently, the cost of food on the bars in that vicinity. At this time the charge for packing from Fort Yale to the Forks [*Lytton*] was 46½ cents, while from Douglas to Lillooet—almost double the distance—it was, by this work, reduced to 18 cents a pound. But the gradual advance from Yale had shown the auriferous nature of all the bars between that point and Lytton. Hence, while the trail to Lillooet afforded access to the upper Couteau [*Thompson*] and Canoe countries, it gave no relief for the territory between Yale and Lytton. The Hudson's Bay Company's Brigade trail, as far as Spuzzum and Anderson River, and the Indian trails, were the lines of communication. In August, Douglas called for proposals to cut a mule trail from Yale by way of Douglas Portage to Spuzzum (sometimes called the Rancheria), and thence for a distance of thirty-five miles along the river. It was to be a trail over which a mule could pack two hundred and fifty pounds.

While this proposal was under consideration, a company of one hundred and sixty men and four hundred mules and horses, in command of David McLaughlin, arrived at Lytton. They had made their rendezvous at Walla Walla. Learning from Mr. Wolfe, a trader of Fort Colville who joined them with a band of cattle, that the Indians were hostile, the party adopted a semi-military organization. Four divisions were formed and placed under the command of James McLaughlin, Hambright, Wilson, and Tucker. A German who lagged behind while crossing the Columbia Plains was taken by the Indians and murdered. Near the boundary line, and on the east side of the Okanagan River, the party met the Indians in force and strongly entrenched. When the latter fired, the whites took shelter behind the rocks and returned the fire. All the afternoon the battle continued. Hurley, Evans, and Rice—three Californians— were killed, and six others wounded. Five horses were also lost in the conflict. During the night the Indians set fire to the grass to burn out the whites, but the latter set counter fires, and both held their positions. In the morning the savages had decamped. From the breastworks which they had erected it was evident that about a hundred Indians had been engaged in the encounter.

A few days later a large band rode down upon the party and endeavored to stampede their animals. Failing in the attempt, peace was made. No sooner had this been arranged than the Indians stole about sixty of Mr. Wolfe's cattle. McLaughlin's men, finding them in the act of jerking the beef, took them prisoners and were about to execute speedy justice upon them when Chief Trader Allen McDonald of Fort Colville most opportunely arrived on the scene. At his intercession the malefactors were released. The whole journey occupied about thirty days. The trail was described as being so bad that one, who had once travelled it, would not desire to do so again.

Immediately after their arrival, one hundred of the mules were sent down the river trail towards Yale. When this news reached Yale, a meeting of the miners was held and about a hundred men volunteered to render the trail by way of Spuzzum and Boston Bar.

They set to work and made the trail as far as Spuzzum so passable that a mule could travel it with a load of two hundred pounds. The Governor took up the work where these volunteers ceased.

From Fort Yale to the Ferry the trail was in fair condition, but the remainder of the distance to Lytton was very rough, full of big logs and difficult places to travel, though loaded mules managed to pass over. By September 7th it was estimated that five hundred mules were packing over this trail from Yale to Lytton.

Besides this trail, there were two others known as the "Lower" and "Upper" Canyon Trails. The former was a rough path carried along a ledge of boulders at the bottom of the canyon, but openly passable when the water was low. The Upper Trail passed from ledge to ledge at a height varying from fifty to eight hundred feet above the river. They connected with the mule trail and afforded short cuts to those whose nerves were strong enough to stand the strain. The test came in rounding the cliffs.

Here the Indians had suspended poles by ropes of deer hide and fibre, and in passing there was nothing for the traveller to grasp. He could only stretch out his arms and clasp the face of the rock, keeping as close to it as possible. If he became dizzy, or made a false step, the pole would swing away and place him in danger of toppling off. Yet the Indians who were accustomed to the work used these two trails for packing in supplies for the miners when the mule trail, owing to its elevation, was blocked with snow. The miners themselves were also obliged to use the same routes, dangerous as they were, and to carry their provisions along this hazardous pathway during a great portion of the year.

Judge Begbie passed over these trails in the following April. He describes them as being: "Utterly impassable for any animal but a man, a goat, or a dog." He adds: "It might, doubtless, be very much improved. In many places a very painful and dangerous ascent and descent of twenty minutes, in the whole course of which the traveller depends almost as much on his hands as on his feet, brings the path to within a few yards of the projecting precipice, through which a few pounds of powder would have made an easy way."

Lieutenant Mayne had no better opinion of these trails through the canyons: "The ground over which the trail passes is the roughest on which I have ever travelled, the greater part of it being over sharp-pointed rocks or granite boulders. Some of the ascents in the Great Canyon, which is six miles long, are from 30° to 60° and nearly perpendicular over the water."

In 1860, the Governor entered upon his road construction policy. He had realized from the beginning that roads were a prime necessity. But mining is proverbially uncertain, and the unstable mining community, rushing hither and thither as reports of rich strikes reached them, kept in doubt the proper line of permanent roadway. However, it was plain that access to the Interior must be given. The first step was to transform the existing trail from Douglas to Lillooet into a wagon road. After Lieutenant Palmer had examined it in May 1859, about a hundred men of the Royal Engineers were employed in improving the portion near Douglas.

In March 1860, Captain [*John Marshall*] Grant, with eighty men of the corps, spent some time endeavoring to deepen the channel through the shoal of Harrison River so as to allow uninterrupted navigation at all stages of the water as far as Douglas. Later this party resumed work on the road. By October, with the assistance of some civilians, they completed it from Douglas to the Twenty-eight Mile House at Little Lillooet Lake in such a manner as to receive the highest encomiums from the Governor. A number of freight wagons were placed on this section, and thus the cost of transportation was again reduced.

In the following year the Royal Engineers continued their work on the same portion, reducing the grades and improving the roadbed. When it was completed Lieutenant Mayne described it as "a wagon road which would be no discredit to many parts of England."

The contract for the Douglas-Lillooet road on the second portage—Lillooet Lake to Anderson Lake, a distance of twenty-four miles—was in August 1861 awarded to Colquhoun & Company. This was to be eighteen feet in width instead of twelve feet. The contractors were unable to complete the undertaking beyond the first eight miles. In August 1861, the contract for finishing it was awarded to Joseph W. Trutch. In October 1861, he had one hundred and fifty men at work and was pressing construction rapidly forward. Between Anderson and Seton Lakes—one and one-half miles—Mr. P. Smith had a tramway in operation by the fall of 1861. From Seton Lake to Lillooet—four miles—the road was built by Mr. Watson and completed by November 1, 1861.

With the opening of navigation in 1862, freight wagons and stages were in operation over the whole extent of the Douglas-Lillooet route. Steamers were plying on the various lakes—the *Marzella* [*Marzelle*] on Lillooet Lake, the *Lady of the Lake* on Anderson Lake, and the *Champion* on Seton Lake.

Taking the hint which the Gold Commissioner at Yale had thrown out, the Governor determined to build a trail along the mountain side from Fort Yale to Spuzzum, and from that point to Boston Bar, following the course of the Fraser at a moderate elevation. As already stated, the Brigade Trail could only be used during about four months in the year. In June 1860, a contract was made with Franklin Way of Spuzzum and Josiah C. Beedy of Yale to build this trail as far as Spuzzum. Messrs. Powers and McRoberts, in the same summer, built the trail from

Spuzzum to Boston Bar at the mouth of Anderson River. When the Governor made a tour of the colony in October 1860, the trail was completed and open for traffic. [*Douglas commented:*] "In riding over the face of these frowning cliffs, which a twelve month ago seemed to defy all efforts at improvement, it was impossible to suppress a feeling of thankfulnes [*sic*] and intense gratification at the successful issue of our labours and their probable influence on the trade and development of the country. The arduous part of this undertaking—excavating the mountain near Yale— was executed entirely by a detachment of Royal Engineers under Sergeant-Major George Cann, and it has been completed in a manner highly creditable to themselves and to the officers who directed the operation."

[*Tolls were placed on the new trails in October 1860. The charge was 25 cents for every 50 pounds. Miners' packs not exceeding 30 pounds and goods that were the property of Natives were exempt from charges. Despite the tolls, the new trails were an immediate success and soon long lines of mules were carefully picking their way along the precipitous slopes of the Fraser Canyon northward to the mines of Cariboo.*]

The mule trains usually consisted of from sixteen to forty-eight animals. No pack saddles were used. Instead a rough sort of leather sack, filled with straw and called an "aparajoe," was girded tightly upon the mule's back. Upon this was lashed the freight (two hundred and fifty or even four hundred pounds), and secured with the celebrated diamond hitch. A bell animal, usually a white mare, led the train. There was no control over the mules when packing, though each knew its place.

Besides a cook and a superintendent, or cargodore, there was a crew, as they were called, consisting of one man for every eight animals. The packers first followed the Brigade Trail from Yale to the crossing of Anderson River, made their way down that river to Boston Bar, thence took an Indian trail over Jackass Mountain to Lytton. When Powers and McRoberts built the trail from Spuzzum to Boston Bar along the left bank of the Fraser, the packers took that route instead of the Brigade Trail. In detail the route was: 1st day, Yale to Spuzzum; 2nd day, Spuzzum to Lake House; 3rd day, Lake House to Thousand Dollar Bill on the top of the hill from Boston Bar; 4th day, Thousand Dollar Bill to Butcher Flat; 5th day, Butcher Flat to Boothroyd Flat; 6th day, Boothroyd Flat to Kanaka Bar; 7th day, Kanaka Bar to Lytton; 8th day, Lytton to Nicomen; 9th day, Nicomen to Cook's Ferry. Four miles beyond Cook's Ferry the Thompson was left and the remainder of the route to Quesnel Forks was made in seventeen or eighteen days. The rate of travel there was about fifteen miles a day.

On this part of the journey there [was] no regular day's travel; the camping places depended upon water and feed for the train. The trip upward occupied about a month; the return a little less. Three trips were made in a season. Nevertheless, packing was the most lucrative of employments. The train soon paid the capital expense, and then great profits were made. Early in 1861 the rate from Yale to the Forks of Quesnel was $1 a pound. From that point to Antler, before the trail was made, Indians packed for 40 cents a pound. The rate fell as soon as pack trains could reach Antler Creek. In the summer of 1861 the charge for packing from Yale to Quesnel Forks had fallen to 40 cents a pound. In July 1861, four hundred and eight pack animals left Yale for the Cariboo mines.

Besides the mule trains, there was introduced into the colony in 1862 another pack animal, a stranger to our climate, the camel. Mr. Frank Laumeister, a prominent merchant and packer, was the originator of the scheme. It was thought that an animal that could subsist on sage brush, carry a thousand pounds, travel thirty or forty miles a day and go from six to ten days without water would be a success. Camels had been used in 1857–58 by the United States government in connection with the army transport service in Texas and Lower California. With this knowledge Mr. Laumeister procured a band of twenty-one.

They [*the camels*] arrived in May 1862, and were at once sent to Douglas to pack on the portages, as the Douglas-Lillooet road was called. Though they could easily carry twice the load of a mule and pick their own forage, they were not entirely satisfactory. The rough, rocky trails with intervals of marsh and muddy ground were unsuitable for animals whose feet were accustomed to sand. Yet they remained in the business of packing for over a year and made regular trips to Cariboo. They were a great annoyance to the mules on the trail; the latter became quite unmanageable when they scented the strange beasts. Several accidents occurred in consequence, litigation arose, and the owners deemed it the part of wisdom to withdraw them from the road. Some of them were brought to the coast and disposed of, but the remainder were taken over to the Thompson River and turned out to spend their declining days far from their Arabian homes. For years they were a source of terror to horses and mules in the vicinity. The last survivor died about 1905.

CHAPTER

5

How the Cariboo Road Was Built

IN OCTOBER 1861, GOVERNOR DOUGLAS, while at Yale, discussed the feasibility of constructing a wagon road along the Fraser to Lytton and thence to Cook's Ferry on the Thompson. The trail built the preceding year to Spuzzum pointed the way. The Governor was much impressed with the plan. Before departing he arranged to let the contract for the portion from Boston Bar to Lytton, a piece of comparatively easy work, with the exception of the part over Jackass Mountain, and ordered a party of the Royal Engineers to survey for a wagon road from Yale to Boston Bar and from Lytton to Cook's Ferry. He also sent out Sergeant [*William*] McColl with another party of Royal Engineers to select a site for a bridge over the Fraser. The scheme so launched—a bold and daring one for a colony of such limited means—meant the overthrow of nature's gigantic barriers. It meant the quarrying of a roadway eighteen feet wide through those immense shoulders of rock that buttress the Cascades for miles along the Fraser's canyons. To provide an easy means of access to Cariboo was, in Douglas's opinion, a paramount duty of Government. Although the labour was Herculean and the distance four hundred miles, yet travel must be rendered easy, the cost of transportation reduced, and thereby the trade of miners secured and retained for the people of the colony.

About the end of October, Sergeant McColl recommended that the river be bridged at a point about one mile below Chapman's Bar, where its width does not exceed two hundred and fifty feet, and that the road be carried along the left bank, easy grades being obtainable (with the one exception of Nicaragua Slide) the whole distance to Boston Bar.

The surveys having been completed and the location of the suspension bridge settled, the work of construction went on apace along the greater part of the distance between Yale and Cook's Ferry. The first six miles were confided to the Royal Engineers. Captain Grant, R.E., with a party of fifty-three sappers, commenced this section in May 1862, and by the following November had completed a road which was described as "an enduring monument of engineering skill and patient toil." From the six-mile post

(Pike's Riffle) to Chapman's Bar (Suspension Bridge), seven miles, the contract was in the name of Thomas Spence. The cost of this portion of the road was $47,000. From Chapman's Bar to Boston Bar, twelve miles, the contract was in the name of Joseph W. Trutch. Work on this section was commenced in May 1862. It was finished during the latter part of the year at a cost of $75,000. In April 1862, after six months' delay, the contract for the road between Boston Bar and Lytton, thirty-two miles, was awarded to Thomas Spence for $88,000.

By the end of June almost four hundred men were employed, and twelve miles had been completed. Though these three contracts were held in individual names, they were really for the benefit of the partnership of Spence and Trutch. In March 1862, tenders were asked for a wagon road eighteen feet wide—this was the width of the whole Cariboo Road—from Lytton, via the Nicomen River, to Cook's Ferry [*Spence's Bridge*], twenty-one miles along the line blazed by the Royal Engineers in the autumn of 1861, to be completed July 15, 1862.

Charles Oppenheimer and Walter Moberly secured the contract. With them was associated Thomas B. Lewis. In May they were advertising for one thousand men for this work. For a time all went well, and great vigour was shown in its prosecution. The first twelve miles were completed to the entire satisfaction of the Government in June 1862. The time for completion was extended and the formal contract signed on August 16, 1862. But the wild rumours of the untold riches of Cariboo made it extremely difficult for the contractors to obtain anything like the proper number of men. In this dilemma, resort was had to Chinese and Indian workmen, but the virulent outbreak of smallpox in 1862 spread consternation and death amongst the latter, cutting off this source of supply.

On September 30th the Government gave notice that unless the number of workmen was increased to three hundred, and the work energetically pressed forward, the contract would be cancelled; and a fortnight later the threatened action was taken. The Government took possession of the finished road, the unfinished work, and all the contractor's tools and outfit to recoup itself for advances made, and later in the season completed the work. Mr. Moberly, one of the contractors, was in charge for the Government.

The Harrison-Lillooet Road, as completed in 1861, terminated on the Fraser River at Cayoosh [*Lillooet*]. Later in that year Gustavus Blin Wright, the most famous of all the road-builders of colonial days, built the forty-seven miles thence to Clinton, sometimes called Cut-off-Valley. On August 16, 1862, the formal contract was made with him covering the construction of a wagon road from Lillooet to Alexandria. The country through which this two hundred and forty-four miles of road was to pass offered but few obstacles.

In May 1862, Mr. Wright was advertising for five

hundred men to work on this road, and by the end of July 1863, it was completed to Soda Creek. When finished a short time later, Billy Ballou, the pioneer expressman, declared: "It is a No. 1 road for any country." Thus the first traversable road to Cariboo, that by way of Lillooet, was in operation in the summer of 1863.

By June 1863, the road from Yale to Cook's Ferry had been completed, with the exception of about one mile in Mr. Trutch's contract between Chapman's Bar and Boston Bar. In that short space, however, were several rocky bluffs, necessitating heavy blasting operations and requiring some two or three months' work to overcome. Notwithstanding the unfinished state of the road, freight in large quantities was transported along it during the early part of 1863.

As far as the ferry at Spuzzum, large mule wagons were used; thence to Cariboo everything was packed on animals' backs. The Indians, who had found lucrative employment in packing upon their backs supplies for the miners, and had even held their own against the mule teams on the rough trails, found themselves unable to compete against the mule teams on the road. Already the price of packing from Yale to Richfield, [on] Williams Creek, which had previously been about 90 cents a pound, had dropped to 50 cents a pound. It was confidently expected that on completion of the road and the advent of wagons, the price would fall to 25 cents. It fell below that figure. In May 1864, it was 15 to 18 cents a pound.

To complete the Yale-Cariboo wagon road there remained, in 1863, to be placed under contract: (1) the suspension bridge to replace the ferry at Spuzzum; (2) a connection between Cook's Ferry and the existing road by way of Harrison-Lillooet-Alexandria, which Mr. Wright had built during that summer; (3) Cook's Ferry, [*which had to*] give place to a traffic bridge across the Thompson. The two first-mentioned works were undertaken and completed in 1863.

On February 2, 1863, an agreement was made whereby Joseph W. Trutch undertook to build a suspension bridge, to be called the Alexandra Bridge, across the Fraser at the point which had been selected by Sergeant McColl in October, 1861. This was the first bridge [*built*] on the suspension principle in either colony [*Vancouver Island and British Columbia*]. The span was over three hundred feet. In the following September the bridge was finished at a cost of about $45,000 and accepted on the examination and report of Lieutenant Palmer. A four-horse team with a load of three tons was driven over as a sort of test, but the deflection was inappreciable, not amounting to more than a quarter of an inch.

The gap between Cook's Ferry and Clinton on the Lillooet-Alexandria road was closed during the summer of 1863. The first nine miles of this portion were built by the Royal Engineers under Lieutenant Palmer. William Hood of Cache Creek performed the remainder of the work, fulfilling his undertaking by August 1863. It was claimed that Hood's road was the best in the colony.

The avidity with which the public grasped the new conditions may be inferred from the fact that in July 1863, before the completion, a traveler reported meeting, between Cook's Ferry and Yale, ten loaded wagons carrying four thousand pounds each and two hundred and fifty pack animals, many of which had four hundred pounds on their backs.

In February 1864, Thomas Spence undertook to build a bridge, known as Spence's Bridge, in the vicinity of Cook's Ferry. The freshet carried away a part of the piers and did considerable damage. When the water subsided the work was resumed and completed late in the fall. The erection of this bridge, which cost about $15,000, was the last link in the chain from Yale to Alexandria. On the strength of the loss by the freshet, Mr. Spence applied to the Legislative Council, in 1868, and obtained an extension of his charter right to collect tolls for two and a half years.

Before passing away from this portion of the subject, reference must be made to the terms on which the roads, both by way of Harrison-Lillooet and by Yale, were constructed. Those portions which were built by the Royal Engineers were directly paid for by the Government of the Colony; the remainder of the Harrison-Lillooet road, as far as Lillooet, was paid for in cash and bonds; the Yale-Cariboo road, as far as Clinton, was also paid for in cash and bonds;

but tolls were payable to the contractors on the Alexandra Bridge, Spence's Bridge, and the whole road from Lillooet to Alexandria for varying periods of five and seven years.

From Alexandria to Quesnel mouth the communication was for a long time by steamboat. The first vessel on this route was the *Enterprise*, built in 1863 by G.B. Wright at a cost of $75,000, the whole of the machinery and boiler plates having been brought two hundred miles on the backs of mules.

Early in 1864 Wright undertook the construction of a wagon road from Quesnel to Cottonwood, on the way to Williams Creek, twenty-six miles. In July there were about one hundred whites and two hundred Chinese at work upon it. The former were mostly miners who had become disheartened with Cariboo and its deep diggings and were anxious to earn money to reach the coast or the Kootenay mines, where shallow diggings, the lodestar of the individual miner, were reported to exist. This portion was completed by September 1864, at a cost of about $85,000.

In 1864, F.J. Barnard put on a line of stagecoaches from Yale and Douglas to Soda Creek. The Cariboo Stage Company, Messrs. Humphrey, Poole, and Johnston, began in 1865 to operate stagecoaches on the newly-finished road from Quesnel to Cottonwood, connecting there with a saddle train for Williams Creek.

The remainder of the road from Cottonwood to Williams Creek was placed under contract in 1865. In June,

Mr. Munro was given the contract as far as Barkerville for $45,000. Late in the fall this was completed and the last link in the chain was forged.

One of the results of the completion of the road was to reduce the freight to Cariboo from 75 cents to 15 cents a pound. But against this advantage the goods were subject to the tolls which have been specified. These levies were no inconsiderable sum, amounting often to more than the first cost of the merchandise. For example, goods for Cariboo were subject to the tonnage tax of $3 per ton on leaving New Westminster; at Yale or Douglas a toll of 1 cent a pound was levied; on the Suspension Bridge a further charge of ⅓ cent per pound; on Spence's Bridge a similar charge; and another toll of 1 cent a pound on the road beyond Lytton and Lillooet—in all $56.33 a ton, or almost 3 cents a pound. When to this was added the freight rate of 15 or 18 cents a pound it will readily be seen that in many instances the cost of transportation doubled or trebled the price of the articles themselves. In 1865, the tolls collected amounted to $80,000; the cost of collection was $12,000.

Although somewhat out of chronological sequence, yet to complete the view of the Cariboo Road the attempt to utilize steam traction engines upon it for the transportation of freight may be mentioned. In 1864, R.C. Janion of Liverpool, W.L. Green of Honolulu, Henry Rhodes, and Joseph W. Trutch obtained permission to use these engines on the Cariboo Road. They were required to introduce three, at least, into the colony by May 1, 1866. The object aimed at was more speedy and cheap conveyance of supplies and material. The rights of the original promoters passed over to F.J. Barnard and J.C. Beedy.

Five of these engines and the necessary wagons were imported from Scotland, together with engineers to operate them. One was duly placed in commission and sent out from Yale with a load of twelve thousand pounds. It succeeded in reaching Spuzzum on the first day, Boston Bar on the second, and the top of Jackass Mountain on the third. There its journey toward Cariboo ended.

The rate of travel had been demonstrated to be no greater than that of the regular freight wagons. On the other hand, the cost was greater, owing to the enormous wear and tear, the expense of operation, and the necessity of strengthening all the bridges on the road. One of the engines was later employed in logging operations carried on by Jeremiah Rogers at Jericho on English Bay, and the remainder were returned to Scotland.

Reaching from Yale, the head of navigation, to the mines of Cariboo, a distance of nearly four hundred miles and solidly and substantially constructed by our infant colony in less than three years, this road was the pride of British Columbia. It was also a source of wonder and admiration to its visitors, who were loud in their expressions of surprise at the daring conception and skilful execution of the work. Here the road was supported by piling, there built upon immense masonry "fills," sometimes on gigantic crib-work, the ruins of which yet remain, sometimes cut through a sheer rock bluff, now almost at the water level, and anon raised to giddy elevations whence the river seemed but a silver ribbon.

As one writer noted: "If we could only look back into the past along that mighty highway, what a strange scene we should behold. Long lines of pack animals, heavy freight wagons, six-horse coaches, with the well-known faces of their passengers, camels and traction engines, an army of men with packstraps, some going, some returning, some successful, many unsuccessful, men drunk and men sober—all sorts and conditions of men—a motley crowd; bustling activity at the rough and ready roadhouses; such was the Cariboo road in the palmy days of its greatness that are no more."

With the completion of the Yale-Cariboo Road there were two conflicting routes to the mines—that which commenced at Douglas and that which commenced at Yale. From Clinton northward these two roads were merged. A great rivalry sprang up between them for the trade of Cariboo. The Douglas route, being the older, had until 1863 a monopoly, or, at any rate, far the greater share of the business. The interested persons, the traders, the roadside house proprietors, the steamboat owners on the lakes, strove energetically to retain it. But natural conditions were unfavourable.

The difficulty [lay] in reaching even Douglas itself,

owing to the shoals of the Harrison River, which necessitated transshipment except during the freshets; thereafter the constant changes from land to water travel, with the incidental delays in making connection with the steamers on the three lakes, soon settled the question in favor of Yale. On that route the freight was landed at all times of the year at Yale and, once placed in the wagons, could be sent through to the mines without any harassing delays. Against this was merely the extra toll on the Suspension Bridge and Spence's Bridge, which, together, only amounted to ⅔ of a cent a pound. From the completion of the road through the canyons, the Douglas route gradually fell into disuse.

6

The First Tourists to the Cariboo

Introduction

From 1858 to 1862, some 40,000 people from around the world were lured to the Fraser River and the Cariboo by the word "gold." All intended to become wealthy through finding nuggets by the pound or establishing hotels, saloons, stores, wayside stopping places and similar businesses. But two men, Dr. Walter B. Cheadle and Lord Viscount Milton, the sixth Earl Fitzwilliam, had a startlingly different reason. As Cheadle later wrote, they travelled "for pleasure," thus becoming the first tourists to visit not only the Cariboo but also to cross Canada.

In the early 1860s, however, Canada was dramatically different from the country it is today. In the east was the

This sketch from Cheadle and Milton's 1865 book, *North-West Passage by Land*, portrays Milton (second from the left) and Cheadle (in the middle) with the Assiniboine guides who accompanied them over the mountains.

province of Canada, which comprised the Maritimes and a slice inland about one-third the size of Ontario and Quebec. In the west were two Crown colonies, Vancouver Island and British Columbia, both governed from England. In between was a massive region called Rupert's Land, the Stikine Territory and the North-Western Territory. Bigger than Europe, this region extended over 2,000 miles from east to west and 1,600 miles from the southern grassland to the Arctic Ocean. It was a massive fur preserve of the Hudson's Bay Company, their small isolated forts the only sign of white habitation.

Milton and Cheadle's journey from Atlantic to Pacific took them over a year. Luck was their companion, especially when they reached the Rockies. They were six weeks battling through 180 miles of wilderness between Mount Robson and Fort Kamloops and almost died of starvation. After they arrived back in England, they recounted their adventures in a book titled *North-West Passage by Land*. It quickly became one of the most popular travel books of the era, selling eight printings, the ninth and final one appearing in 1891. Although both names appeared as authors, it was generally known that Cheadle had written the book, basing it on his journal of their venture.

North-West Passage by Land

For some 70 years the journal was known mainly to Cheadle's heirs. Then in 1931, A.G. Doughty and Gustave Lanctot of the Public Archives of Canada prepared the journal for publication, calling it *Cheadle's Journal of a Trip across Canada 1862–63*. In the introduction, they describe Cheadle and Milton's travels and the considerable trials they faced before reaching the Cariboo:

> Walter Butler Cheadle was the first to traverse the whole country from the St. Lawrence to the Pacific simply "for pleasure," for the sheer enjoyment of seeing new lands, hunting the buffalo and visiting the gold regions of Cariboo. He was then twenty-seven years of age, in the prime of his manhood, a sturdy son of Old England and a former

Cambridge oarsman. This may explain his adventurous propensities . . . For one must remember that in 1862 the Prairie and Pacific provinces were really a wild West, a country without roads or settlements, and deserted with the exception of distant fur-trading posts and occasional roaming Indians.

The author, Walter Butler Cheadle, with his companion, Lord Milton, left Liverpool in June 1862 and reached Quebec on the 2nd of July. By boat they proceeded at once to Toronto, visiting Niagara Falls, and then by railway through Detroit and Chicago to La Crosse, on the Mississippi. Here, they boarded a steamer which conveyed them to St. Paul, whence a journey by rail brought them to St. Anthony. From that place, they travelled by stage to Georgetown on the Red River. Here they took to the canoe and reached Fort Garry on the 7th of August.

Soon the actual difficulties of the journey began. Equipping themselves with necessary food, arms and utensils, they purchased horses, secured reliable half-breed guides and left Fort Garry on August 23rd for the Prairies. Their first stop was at Fort Ellice on the Assiniboine and their next at Fort Carlton, on the North Saskatchewan, which they reached on the 26th of September.

The season was now well advanced and therefore Cheadle and Milton went into winter quarters near White Fish Lake, at a place called Jolie or Belle Prairie, about eighty miles from Carlton, where they remained till the 3rd of April 1863. On that date, they returned to Carlton. Securing new guides and provisions they made preparations for the most difficult task of their journey, the crossing of the Rockies. Three days later, they started on their daring enterprise, stopping at Fort

Pitt and later at Fort Edmonton, posts of the Hudson's Bay Company on the North Saskatchewan. On the 3rd of June, the party left Edmonton heading for the Rockies, having decided to cross the mountains by way of the Yellowhead Pass, at that time a very little known route.

Here they faced an exceedingly arduous part of the trip. With a weak party and no experience of local mountain conditions, they reached Jasper House on June 29th and Yellowhead Pass, July 17th. Difficulties soon increased. Well-nigh impassable routes along the Thompson River owing to steep rocky hills, close forests and fallen timber, delayed their advance. A diminishing quantity of food, scarcity of game, the subsequent loss of provisions, instruments and horses, added to their hardships and privations, and reduced them to the necessity of killing their pack-horses to save the party from starvation. But thanks to an indomitable spirit and the resource of their French half-breed guide, they finally reached Kamloops on August 28th. But their condition was pitiable. Their clothes were in tatters, their faces were gaunt and haggard, and their bodies in a state of almost complete exhaustion from exposure, fatigue and lack of nourishment.

At Kamloops the travellers re-victualled and proceeded to New Westminster and Victoria. Now they carried out the last part of their programme, by taking a trip by boat and stage to the gold regions of the Cariboo as far as Richfield.

Having taken over 14 months on their overland journey, Milton and Cheadle arrived in Victoria on September 19. They stayed in Victoria for 10 days, then left by sternwheel steamer for New Westminster, beginning their trip to the

Cariboo. At New Westminster they attended a land sale where Milton, "carried away by the excitement," bought seven lots ranging in size from three to nine acres, paying from $100 to $160 each. Today the lots are part of downtown New Westminster and worth many times more per foot than Milton paid for a nine-acre block.

On Thursday, October 1, they boarded the sternwheel steamer *Hope* for the first part of their journey up the Fraser River to Harrison Lake. During most of the night the sternwheeler "wooded up," or took on the four-foot chunks of cordwood used for fuel. As Cheadle noted, they got "but little sleep in our narrow berths, for which they charged us $2 each."

On their upward journey they travelled via the Harrison–Lillooet route, which bypassed the Fraser Canyon by a series of lakes and rivers. Late in 1858, a trail had been slashed around the Fraser Canyon to Lillooet, and in 1860 it was widened to a wagon road. From Port Douglas on Harrison Lake the road led overland 38 miles to Lillooet Lake. Here a steamer, *Lady of the Lake*, connected to a 30-mile road that led from Lillooet to Anderson Lake. Service on 19-mile-long Anderson Lake was provided by another sternwheeler, *Marzelle*. From Anderson Lake, a mile and a half of road led to 23-mile Seton Lake and another steamer, *Champion*. From Seton Lake a road led 3 miles to Lillooet. Then, in 1861, Gustavus Blin Wright began work on 47 miles of road from Lillooet to a point that became known as Clinton.

But this route wasn't satisfactory. The road being built by Wright climbed over a 4,000-foot mountain, and grades were steep and hazardous. From Port Douglas to Lillooet, freight had to be transferred from steamer to wagon and wagon to steamer at least eight times, each transfer resulting in an increase in freight rates. It was evident that this route would never serve as the main thoroughfare to Cariboo. Fortunately there were men of vision at the head of government. In 1861, Governor Douglas outlined a plan as bold and imaginative as anything previously undertaken in North America. It called for construction of an 18-foot wagon road north 400 miles through the rock barrier of the Fraser Canyon and across the lonely wilderness miles to the goldfields. Considering that the permanent population of the colony was under 7,000, the project was a stupendous undertaking.

Work on the Cariboo Wagon Road began in October 1861 and by September 1863 had been completed from Yale in the Fraser Canyon 300 miles to Soda Creek in the Cariboo. The Harrison Lake–Lillooet route was soon abandoned. Milton and Cheadle, however, went to the Cariboo via the Lillooet route and returned on the new wagon road through the Fraser Canyon.

The following excerpts from Walter Cheadle's journal relate the travellers' experiences during their six-week trip to the Cariboo's golden creeks.

Cheadle's Journal, October 2 to December 3, 1863

Friday, October 2nd—Going before daybreak, having anchored most of the night; a great flat boat full of hay lashed alongside & delaying our progress, so that we did not reach Douglas until 6 o'clock. 45 miles from New Westminster. Douglas [*Harrison*] Lake 45 miles long; immense numbers of salmon splashing about in shallows of rapid in Harrison River. Indian boys in canoes spearing them now in bad season. Bill on boat $10 each for 3 meals, passage & bed. Douglas a vile hole in hollow formed by continuation of lake basin up to hill beyond lake; put up at Macdonald's; wretched supper of pork & liver. Miners gambling & drinking. Yankees preponderating; scarcity of women. Silver mine on Harrison Lake; talk of working it.

Saturday, October 3rd—Find stage will not go till Monday. Walk up to inquire of Mr. Gaggin the Judge if there are any other means of getting forward. Regular jolly Irishman from Cork; kindly promises to lend Milton a horse if I can find another. Agree to start on horseback tomorrow. Introduced to a Captain Nunn, very stout & barefaced, small featured; & Dr. Sylvester a handsome young fellow with slightly grey hair & shaky hand. Gaggin told us of miners & Chinamen coming down in canoes without their heads. Barrett Lennard never came further than Harrison Lake into British Columbia, & Macdonald (another author) never beyond Langley. Delayed us with beer. About 5, stage came in with 10 miners. Prisoner brought in. Going up to see Gaggin, met a Sywash prisoner who had escaped, just recaptured, shot in the neck by constable altho' he did not resist; trotted along with string to the ring of his gyves [*shackles*].

Sunday, October 4th—After sundry beers & procrastinations we set out. Gaggin having found a mule for me for which I had to pay $10 for the 29 miles. The Judge accompanied us on a grey horse which had been left behind by a Mr. Flinn gone down to Victoria. "The Judge" turned out a "whale for drink," & we pulled up at every wayside house to refresh; as we started late our chance of getting thro' looked small; dined at the 10-mile house where we were so strongly advised by the Governor to have a feed; & a very nice clean dinner we had. Kept by a German named Perrin. From there we trotted on to the 16-mile house kept by an old Scotch ship's-carpenter named Wake, & finding it late, we resolved to stay the night & ride forward in time for the steamer in the morning. Gaggin & I had two jugs of mulled claret which made us sleep like tops.

Monday, October 5th—Off at 7 to catch the steamer at 12. At the 20-mile house there is a hot spring & baths; rude wooden affairs. Water a slight smell of sulphuretted hydrogen, & said by bath proprietor to contain common salt & nitrate of soda; reputation for cure of rheumatism; the water

Cariboo accommodation was often very basic, with up to 30 men sharing a room. Cheadle noted of the roadhouse portrayed in this sketch: "The only bed was the floor . . . at one end a large open chimney, and, at one side, a bar counter, behind which are shelves with rows of bottles containing the vilest of alcoholic drinks."
NORTH-WEST PASSAGE BY LAND

runs out of the solid rock at the foot of the hill in a small stream the size of one's finger; hot enough to boil an egg; similar spring at the foot of Harrison Lake. [*This is the site of today's Harrison Hot Springs Resort & Spa.*] My mule 'Yank' falling lame, I rode on, leaving Milton & Gaggin at the 24-mile house refreshing. Arrived at foot of the little lake (29-mile house) an hour before the steamer started, dined

& waited in vain for Milton & Gaggin; the steamer at last starting & leaving us in the lurch; much annoyed at thus losing a day. Presently stage came in from Douglas, bringing only one passenger, Mr. Flinn, whose horse Gaggin had impressed to ride along with us. Also "Hard Cussie" & another fellow of the well-known "Hard Cussie" claim. About 4 o'clock Milton & "The Judge" arrived, the latter having met some friends at the last house & gone through ½ doz. of stout!

Introduced to Mr. Flinn who has a farm & the ferry at Lillooet & kindly offered me his horse to ride over the portages. Gaggin & the landlady (an Irishwoman) had chaff all the evening; very nice clean beds. Country between Douglas & Little Lillooet Lake thickly wooded; very little farming country; flat patches of small extent; usual gorges & hills; mostly rocky ground.

Passed Summit Lake, water flowing in opposite directions supplying 2 rivers.

Tuesday, October 6th—Steamer brought in 2 prostitutes, white woman & negress, having spent the season in Cariboo (made fortunes). Over Little Lillooet Lake in tiny steamer, then portage past rapids (some ½ mile) which are not passable at lower water; & then in fine steamer "Prince of Wales" over Great Lillooet Lake to Pemberton, a miserable rocky place. Gaggin accompanied us. Continual liquorings up, which Milton & I shirked as well as we could. Lakes surrounded with lofty rocky mountains sparsely wooded with pine & poplar. Arrived at dark.

Wednesday, October 7th—Bid a kind adieu to Gaggin, & then forward 24 miles to Anderson Lake; pretty good road & usual scenery; a little farming land called The Meadows 2 or 3 miles from Pemberton. Milton rode Gaggin's mare, & I Flinn's grey, both capital hackneys, & we went thro' at a great pace. Flinn borrowed a horse, & "Charley Chapman" the owner of the steamer, accompanied us. For dinner we stayed at the house halfway owned by a Virginian of the name of Ketterel. He had only been there a year. There is a fine open flat of I suppose 100 acres partly under cultivation, such good open land is rare. He bought at 2,000 dollars, & the first year's crops paid the purchase . . . Ketterel was an ardent Southerner & the most gentlemanly American we have met, very quiet & does not "blow." He & Flinn praised the Governor highly, & assured us that, were there to be an election for the office, he would have 99% of the votes. Ketterel had two pretty little daughters whom he evidently idolized & the youngest who could hardly talk informed us lispingly that she was "for Jeff Davis," & when she went home she should "fight the Yankees." [*The American Civil War was fought from 1861 to 1865.*] Rode on rapidly to Anderson where we slept; Nice clean house kept by Frenchman; meals $1 each. Beds $1. Horses $1 per bed.

Thursday, October 8th—Away at 6.30 over Anderson Lake; in slow old steamer which took 3 hours to do some 16 miles; then portage of a mile to Seaton Lake where we had a fast boat which brought us across the lake in 1½ hours. The scenery on this lake is finer than the others, the mountains being higher, steeper & more rugged, descending nearly perpendicularly into the water. The brilliant yellow & red autumn tints contrasting with the dark green & black of the pines, & the bright green of the poplars, together with the varied shades of the rocks were more beautiful than I ever saw before. From Seaton, Milton & Flinn rode in. We loaded a "Lywarle" with our small baggage, & I walked in the 4 miles to Lillooet, a town of one street on one of the terraces of the Fraser. Very fair accommodation at the Stage Hotel.

Introduced us to "Judge Elliot," a pleasant little man who had crossed the Atlantic with Milton when he came out to New York before. He invited us to his house & introduced us to Mrs. Elliot, a very ladylike woman, with whom I was rather smitten, having a most remarkable likeness to Mrs. Tylor in both face & manner. In evening met Dr. Walker just arrived from Cariboo . . . Very jolly fellow indeed; in Cariboo 5 months; gave us very unpromising news; snow, slush, mire already; not likely to get in with horses if at all. Miners phrases, "You bet," "You bet your gumboots!" "Your bottom dollar," "putting on frills," "piling the agonies," "getting into the mines," & "Caved in," "Played out."

Friday, October 9th—Resolve to go by stage tomorrow. Rather a disturbed night. A half tipsy miner burst into our bedroom & swore it was his, & that it had 3 beds in before-time. I assured him that it had now only two, & was not his & he made tracks; then at daybreak they rowed us out to ask if we were going on to Seaton by the stage; later on, the bottom of my bed which consisted of nothing but laths nailed on to the frame gave way & I came bump on to the floor, & was compelled to move the mattress on to the floor at the side & try again. Two men passing my door & seeing my boots outside where I had put them in vain hope of their being cleaned a little called out "Who's that d—d d—l, putting on the frills he is?" After breakfast wrote up my notes, & talked with Walker. A poor fellow nearly dying of Cardiac dropsy came in yesterday evening & was very thankful to get me to prescribe for him; better today. Dined with Elliot & met Reverend Brown the parson here, & author of the essay. After leaving there visited Subsheriff Hudson, newly married man; Walker & Flinn there; nice music, "Glorious Apollo" & other glees. "O wert thou in the cauld blast," reminding me of home; not in bed till 12.

Saturday, October 10th—Up at 7, hoping to start at eight & make the 47-mile house (Clinton). But did not leave until 10.30, owing to packing of freight ¾ ton, & only 3 passengers viz. ourselves & Mr. Hall, the Canadian whose horse had foundered over Flinn's ferry and along hilly road mostly cut out of side of mountains & narrow. Our Jehu [*driver*] a Yankee, drove well & rattled us down the hills; cranky stage, & overweighted, (nearly a ton), & if anything should give way, why, over the precipice. Fraser River scenery. Stayed for night at 15-mile house; wretched place, no fire, no beds. Milton slept under the counter, I alongside it, Hall on the top; 4 or 5 miners along the floor.

Sunday, October 11th—Under way about 7. Passed Judge Begbie on horseback. Everybody praises his just severity as the salvation of Cariboo & terror of rowdies. After about 10 miles come to Captain Martley's roadside house; has a ranch near & flourishing. Then up the Pavilion mountain with a tremendous ascent, stage road winding along side of hill, but we walked straight up the mountain side, awfully steep & killing; I think 5000 feet above level. Extraordinary appearance of mountain slope on east of creek at bottom, as if waves of land beginning half way down in small waves, & gradually increasing to larger billows towards the bottom. Volcanic eruption or water? 3 miles along level top brought us to 29-mile house where we got fair dinner; passed numerous returning miners & pack trains. Then after ascending still higher, commence descent of Pavilion by "rattlesnake grade," the most dangerous carriage road I ever saw; the road turns 6 times, is very narrow except at the turns, the mountain side terrifically steep. We rattled down at a fearful pace, a wheel coming off, the brake giving way, or a restive horse

A sketch of Rattlesnake Grade on 4,000-foot-high Pavilion Mountain, where Cheadle and Milton passed one of the camels used for packing to Cariboo.

being almost certain death. At the bottom a lake; at the further end a farm; better land; level road all the way along a valley up to 47-mile house, junction of Lytton & Lillooet roads; several large ranches; only hay, oats, & vegetables grown. Passed a magnificent camel grazing alongside of road; one of the two brought out, first tried in California & then here; failures in both countries. Met Mr. Smith the packer at Clinton; horse given in.

Monday, October 12th—Thro' level country of "cypree" [*conifers*] & lakes to 70-mile house for dinner, & forward to 84 [*84-mile post*] to sleep. Miserable teams, horses wretchedly thin & one lame. Passed this morning a curious chasm in the earth 300 or 400 yards wide height 200 or 300 feet perpendicular. Valley sides as if cut with knife, commencing in a gradual depression & ending abruptly in a valley to the south. Passed the stage going down, full; learnt that the horses for next relay at 84 were still lost; therefore no going on beyond there tonight! & the same horses to go on 17 miles tomorrow! Cameron said to be coming down with 540 lbs weight of gold! real weight 630 lbs, 40 or 50 miners on foot; several mule pack trains. Last porter at 70-mile house 1¼ dollar per pint bottle!

Tuesday, October 13th—Started late as we had only 16 miles to do. Came on heavy rain, giving us a good soaking before arrival, cleared up after. Afternoon to spend here at 100-mile house for want of horses. Met express waggon here. Express left mouth of Quesnel yesterday morning at 6; since then 60 miles by steamer & 78 by waggon! On the road passed a covered waggon which they told us conveyed a sick miner; found out on our arrival at 100-mile house that it was the man who cut his throat a week ago & had been lying there ever since; now sent down to Lillooet for Doctor. The man is mad. All day thro' high table land thickly wooded with small 'cypree,' sandy, rocky & barren. To 100-mile house descended for nearly 3 miles to low ground; apparently better soil; a little open land & scattered poplars, rather reminding one of the Saskatchewan. Three of the 4 Indians condemned to death for murder of 7 whites (which they confessed) are said to have escaped, their jailor taking them out into the woods with him unfettered, & left them there to wait for his return whilst he went to change his boots.

Wednesday, October 14th—Now out of high land with a series of valleys continued from that of last night, strongly resembling 'park-like' country of Saskatchewan; numerous streams & lakes; hills thickly timbered with pines. Along here many "ranches" where oats, barley & vegetables seem to grow pretty well but very short in the straw. Only these "bottoms" that seem at all likely to repay a farmer. At night passed the spot where Clegg was murdered [*Thomas Clegg was shot in August 1863 by a robber named George Storm* *(alias William Armitage), who was later hanged at Lillooet for the crime]*, not ¼ mile from the next house. Thro' road & down hill to Davidson's (150-mile post), a large square unfinished house; billiard room; lots of geese, ducks & chickens. All kinds of vegetables. Mr. Davidson was exceedingly kind & hospitable, as also Mr. Hudson, brother of the man we met at Lillooet. Gave us some very good Hudson's Bay port to supper. Davidson has an extensive farm here & makes money fast, although he says farming land is not first rate & scarce.

Thursday, October 15th—My Birthday, but I forgot to keep it. A long ride with tired horses; dined at Frank Way's 114-mile, he has farm of valley 4 miles long & ¼ wide; over 200 acres; a considerable part of this growing oats & barley which is cut principally for hay. Then, leaving the valleys, we crossed timbered hills, descending by a sinuous & very steep road into the valley of the Fraser once more at Soda Creek to wait here, where there were a few houses, for the steamer at noon tomorrow. House kept by a Yankee. All 'Docs' & 'Caps.'

Friday, October 16th—Steamer came in about 2'clock bringing a host of miners 2 of whom were very drunk & continued to imbibe every 5 minutes; during the time we stayed in the house they must have had 20 drinks. The swearing was something fearful. After we had been on board a short time the Captain finding out who we were, gave us the use of his cabin, a comfortable little room, & supplied us with cigars & a decanter of cocktail, also books & papers. We were fetched out every few minutes to have a drink with some one, the Captain taking the lead by standing champagne all round. We had some dozen to do before supper; no one the least affected, Milton & I shirking in quantity. The 'Cap' told us the boat was built on the river, all the timber sawn by hand, the shaft in 5 pieces packed up on mules, cylinders in two, boiler plates brought in same manner. Boat cost $75,000!

Saturday, October 17th—As we did not leave Soda Creek until 4 & the boat makes very slow progress against the powerful current we had to anchor for night after doing only some 10 miles, & then delayed by the dense fogs which prevail on the river in the early morning at this season. Passed Fort Alexander about 10. No great trade there now; depot of furs from the north; 20 miles from Soda Creek. Country more level & under usual Fraser benches, & low wooded hills; river banks sandy; few rocks; River about size of Saskatchewan at Edmonton; Coal found on banks. Continually called out to have a drink.

Sunday, October 18th—Arrived about 9, at Quesnel mouth, a little collection of about 20 houses on the wooded banks of the Fraser. Quesnel at the north side of the Fort.

Large new stores & cards all lying about the street. A drizzling rain all day. We made up our pack & set out. Captain Done met us in street half seas over [*intoxicated*] & insisted to treat us to champagne, etc., at every bar in the place. At last escaped & walked to 4-mile house where we found Hall & another man who had started before us waiting for us. We stayed there all night. Packers playing cards. Proprietor one of the Canadians who had come overland & down the Fraser last year. Gave fearful account of hardships especially on the raft.

[*The man who rafted down the Fraser River was among a group of some 150 men, a pregnant woman and her three children who in 1862 trekked from eastern Canada to the Cariboo. The group became know as the Overlanders. On June 2, 1862, they left Fort Garry (now Winnipeg) in ox-drawn Red River carts. The first 900 miles to Fort Edmonton they covered fairly quickly, but for much of the route westward from Fort Edmonton there wasn't even a trail. They abandoned their carts and used horses and oxen as pack animals. At Tête Jaune Cache, near Mount Robson, the group split up, some deciding to build huge rafts and challenge the Fraser River, others choosing the Thompson. Several were drowned in the rapid-strewn waterways. In all, the overland trek took three months. The venture was summarized by one of them with the words: "Our mining tools were the only articles . . . that we found to be unnecessary."*]

Monday, October 19th—On foot to Smith's, 2 miles beyond the Cottonwood. Awful trail, nothing but stumps, roots & mud up to the ankles. Saw 6 horses lying dead in the road, hundreds probably a little way off in bush. Thro' nothing but small pines & poplars. Tall 'Maine' man killed 2 martens which crossed the road & we treed, and 2 partridges with his revolver. Very tired and footsore tho' only 20 miles. Milton got thro' famously, walking in moccasins!

Tuesday, October 20th—Sharp frost. Mudholes frozen. Big boots excruciating. Milton & I each picked up a pair of cast away gumboots on the road & left our own at houses till return; 14 miles to dinner & 6 more after to Beaver Pass where we found the Gold Escort & 40 miners; 12 dead horses & mules on the road. I had an awful cold, sore heels & pack of 30 lbs which I found too heavy before dinner. Awful night last night; wind blowing thro' cracks in walls & floor; only one blanket apiece; 20 men in room; one afflicted with cramp in his leg which brought him on his feet swearing every ½ hour. Milton & another talking in their sleep; rest snoring; my nose running; little sleep.

Wednesday, October 21st—In the morning passed along Lightning Creek to Van Winkle; Milton walked very well; my heels very sore; snow getting deeper up to 3 inches. Called at Irishwoman's named Edwards, 3 miles short of Van Winkle, & had a cup of coffee for which she charged us

½ dollar each. Passed Welsh Company's claim which had stopped working on account of ice having broken wheel. [*The "wheel" was a huge water wheel that ran a pump to keep the mine shaft dry.*] At Van Winkle about a dozen houses (Lightning Creek). Passed on 2 miles further to a house where we got a capital dinner, beefsteak pie & beefsteak & onions & pancakes! a long weary walk winding along hill sides past the Bald mountain into William's Creek. Milton held out well walking like a man, carrying his hat slung like a pack although there was frost. At dusk we arrived at Richfield, the first part where gold was struck on this creek, & it was quite dark before we reached Cameron Town below, passing thro' Barkerville or Middle town. The whole 3 towns extending almost continuously down the creek for a mile, & containing about 60 or 70 houses apiece. This spring were only 3 or 4 houses at Cameron Town! Our path was a difficult one over endless sluices, flumes & ditches, across icy planks & logs, all getting tumbles, gum-boots being very treacherous. Putnam the 'Maine man,' took us to his home & treated us, recommending Mr. Cusheon's as a good place to stay at. They gave us a good supper & plenty of blankets.

Thursday, October 22nd—Got up late, being very stiff & sore. In afternoon, Cusheon took us to Cameron Co.'s hut & introduced us to Steele & the other 3 partners of the Cameron Co. except Cameron & Stevenson who had gone down; they treated us to brandy & water & then took us down to view the operations below. The shaft about 30 feet down thro' gravel & clay to bedrock of slate. Numerous shafts all supported by timber & very closely roofed in with flat crosspieces. Wet, damp, dark & gloomy; the shafts being in many parts very low, the "pay dirt" not being extensive perpendicularly. At the bottom shaft the pay dirt was best high up; at the upper end, down close to the bedrock; they kindly helped us to wash out two pans which yielded some beautiful gold to the value of $21, nearly 1⅓ oz, we could see the nuggets lying in the gravel before loosened out by the pick! The claim was bought for a mere nothing, & the thing quite a fluke. Steele showed me about $1000 of gold in a bag, & the Company's books, showing weekly expenses averaging 7000 dollars, the yield being generally from 40 to 112 oz. per shaft (of which there were 3) per day or on to $29,000 per week! over 100 feet of claim yet quite untouched. Steele very kind and intelligent.

Friday, October 23rd—Got up very late, & towards noon walked up the mile to Richfield to see Mr. Cox, a capital fellow. Fat, tall, thick set fellow with very short coat, large features, retiring forehead, no whiskers & large moustache very German; but not in manner. Delicately polite, gentlemanly & jolly. Captain FitzStubbs came in. What a name! had been in army, came out with Barrett Lennard, now speculating in claims. Stayed there until ½ past 4 & on getting back to Cusheon's we found they had eaten our dinner.

A sketch of the famous Cameron claim at Williams Creek.
NORTH-WEST PASSAGE BY LAND

We had however a very nice one in adjacent house of mother-in-law & daughter who treated us hospitably. Steele invited us to Miner's cabin to have a pipe & we got much information from him.

Saturday, October 24th—FitzStubbs took us to visit the Caledonian claim; did not go down himself for fear of dirtying his coat! Two or three proprietors took us round & helped Milton to wash a pan of dirt which produced nearly an ounce of very coarse gold. The shafts in this mine were very low & wet, the pay dirt being not of great depth. Then had lunch in miners' hut & smoked pipes with them. A large portion of this mine yet unworked. On return were introduced to Mr. Raby, a Cornishman & proprietor of the Raby claim. Also Mr. Courtney, a lawyer from Dublin; wonderful number of Irishmen. Raby took us down the "Raby claim" & showed us some rich pockets of gold. The dirt visibly full of it & we could see the 'plums,' the bits of gold in the face of the cutting. The place where we found this "pocket" was under a large boulder & this is where they are usually met with. And it is easy to understand how, when the boulder was lying in what was then the bed of the creek, & the water rippling past it, the gold would lodge in the crevices under the stone. Mr. Raby picked out a few lumps of the rich dirt, as much as would fill a quart pot perhaps, & Milton washed it. There was about an ounce. The Raby claim is very extensive, 1,000 feet, the pay dirt very extensive, being found high above the bed rock as well as on it, the claim being already worked on drifts 12 feet high in some places; gold has also been found plentifully in the gravel above the drifts & Mr. Raby expects to work this from the surface after the drifts are worked out. Enough to last & pay highly for 3 years. The gold seems evidently to have been washed down the old bed of the stream. The difficulty is to find out where the bed of the creek originally was, & the only way seems to be by following the lead. Claims are sometimes taken up & worked on the present bed, & it is found that the "lead" is not there; it passes right into the hill perhaps on one side or the other of the narrow valley; some slide, or volcanic eruption having changed the course of the stream.

We heard of the Dillon & Currie claim where 102 lbs. of gold were taken out as result of 8 hours work! The Wattie shaft where, out of 100 feet of which it consisted, $120,000 were taken, leaving over $70,000 clear profit. Talking to one of the miners, he remarked, "Well, Doctor, I've the greatest respect for both the professions of law & medicine; but its a curious fact that in this creek last year we had neither lawyers nor doctors, & we lived without litigation & free from illness. This year there has been a large influx of both lawyers & doctors, & there has been nothing but lawsuits & deaths in the place!" The appearance of William's Creek (so named from William Dietz, a Prussian, the discoverer) is merely a narrow valley shut in by pine clad hills, the edges & bottom partially cleared & covered with wooden huts, flumes, waterwheels, windlasses, shafts, ditches & tunnels. In the evening went with Stuart, the Cameron Co.'s foreman, to see a Scotchwoman who possessed the most beautiful specimen of native gold I have yet seen. Not more than 2 or 3 oz. but like the most perfectly frosted jeweler's gold & of fantastic shape.

Sunday, October 25th—Did but little till afternoon, when Mr. Greer called & took us up to Richfield to call at his cabin to view some 'specimens.' I am already beginning to hate the name. But these were very fine, one nearly 6 oz. the other 7 oz. Both from Loughea; frosted looking bright gold with quartz. He kindly gave us several nice nuggets from the Greer claim on this creek. Introduced to Dr. Black practising here & who promised to go over to Loughea tomorrow with us, 3 miles from this. Dined with "Judge" Cox who was exceedingly pleasant. Present Courtney, a young Canadian, & an Englishman whose names I did not catch. A jolly evening, & home by bright moonlight in the snow.

Monday, October 26th—Went over with Black to Loughea. He was very pleasant, having seen a great deal of mining in Australia. Loughea very like William's Creek, only smaller scale; 4 claims working, "Sage Miller," Vaughan, Crane's & another. Pays well, & beautifully fine gold; all done by tunnelling. Milton bought $37 worth of gold from Miller, I contented myself with $10. Miller had been all over the world, California, Australia & up the Amazon which he describes as a magnificent country; found gold (flower) in pan. Had pleasant walk over the hill back to William's Creek 3 miles. The great wants here are capital & steam power. Waterwheels freeze up early. Currie & another are now bringing up engines by the first sleighs. "Mr. Dixie," a nigger barber from Tennessee, was introduced to Milton, & as he said he should die happy if he could only shave a real live lord, he is to operate on Milton tomorrow.

Tuesday, October 27th—Went to Bowling Alley with Cusheon, & he & I licked Milton. Thence to see Mr. Raby of whom Milton bought 2 oz gold & I $10 of specimens.

Witnessed washing up of one shaft Raby claim, shift & a half (15 hours), over $4,000! A preserved meat tin case full. At 6 went up to the Hospital the other side of the creek on the top of the hill. Found there Courtenay, Mr. Blenkinsopp, an old H.B. Chief Trader now mining, Mr. Cocker, manager of Macdonald's bank here, Dr. Bell, a G.P., Brown, a young Irishman assisting Dr. Black, & Billy Farren, a successful miner in the Caledonia Claim, a rough boisterous Irishman who had been a sailor. Also Janet Morris, a Scotchwoman, fair, fat & forty, the wife of a man who keeps a store, & who came to make the plum-pudding etc. & of course sat down & dined with us. Champagne ad-lib, & Dr. Bell rapidly became maudlin. He was a little smooth-faced man in dress coat, with large mouth & white teeth always smiling, under some obligation to the FitzWilliam family under whom his father is tenant in Northamptonshire. He rose after the first glass before we had got to pudding & proposed in the most fulsome & absurd manner Milton's health & the Aristocracy of England. "Gentlemen, Dr. Black invited me here to meet a noble scion of the noblest house in England. I don't exaggerate when I say so. I can't exaggerate. I feel grateful to Dr. Black, deeply grateful for asking me here to meet the 'noble scion' of one of the noblest houses England ever produced. It is a proud day for all of us & for this creek; it is the commencement of a new era," etc. etc, quite nauseous, & he continued to propose toasts. Interlude, "He's a jolly good fellow" & sentiments, all full of the "Noble Scion." Then

Dr. Black overflowing with loyalty, laying his hand upon his heart & willing to die at once for his Queen & country; proposing the health of Her Majesty. Interlude "God save the Queen." My health. Interlude "He's a jolly good fellow" etc. We then adjourned to the kitchen & had more healths; songs. And then Janet presented Milton very prettily with a handsome nugget (25 dollars) for him to give his mother from her. After which in a "gushing" speech Black presented Milton with a large gold ring made on the Creek out of "never sweat" gold worth some $50. Billy Farren then gave me a nice gold & quartz specimen, & Janet another. After all which Dr. Bell essayed several speeches but was sung down by the company in Auld Lang Syne, & after sitting half asleep for some time made a bolt for the door which he thought was next to the chimney, & was led off to bed by Mr. Brown. He rolled off with a crash twice during the evening, cutting his head against the stove. The dinner was held in the Hospital ward, the only patient a poor devil with anascara being covered up with a piece of baize hanging from the wall. We had whist & 7 up pitch, after which supper & hot grog with numerous arguments about the mining laws until two o'clock when I persuaded Milton to come home. Both quite sober.

Wednesday, October 28th—Milton went down another shaft of the Caledonia, & I, sick of going down in buckets, & crouching along drifts, walked on to Richfield & had pipe

During their travels in the Cariboo, Cheadle and Milton observed miners washing for gold, as shown in this sketch.

NORTH-WEST PASSAGE BY LAND

with the Judge where Milton joined me shortly; we entered into negotiations to borrow $500 from Cox, who was very kind & lent it us gladly; we were already out of cash, having spent $2000 since leaving Victoria, & Cox said that was very moderate indeed! To call next day for the money.

Thursday, October 29th—Went with Black to call on 'Janet' & bade her an affectionate goodbye. Introduced to Mr. Stenhouse, who had been a man of property in England, ruined by a 'Derby,' afterwards made a large fortune as stage coach proprietor in Australia which he again lost, & is now living on speculations & his wits here; a very coarse vulgar but amusing man withal. Volunteers to go down with us tomorrow. Called at the Judge's for cash. Snowstorm; now nearly a foot of snow here, but not cold except at night when it is down to 5°. In evening Black called & took us into Jem O'B's of the Caledonia to drink whiskey punch.

Friday, October 30th—Bade goodbye to Cusheon & Cameron Town, called & bid adieu to Cox. Our bill for 8 days was 78 dollars each, & very moderate for the place. An Irishman caught us up & walked in company as far as the Edwards, 4 miles from Van Winkle. He amused me keeping a constant talk all the way. He was a cattle driver & said he knew the whole country well. Had hunted cattle nearly up to the head of the Fraser & round to Fort George, starting from Antler Creek! a few nights ago in danger from a pack of wolves at Cottonwood. Out on horseback. Climbed into a tree & set fire to the gum etc., & they eventually cleared off. At Edwards we found Stuart (Cameron foreman) & Mathieson (partner in Victoria firm & in claims here); they were on their way to look at two men prospecting the 'Ayrshire Lass' claim on Lightning above on the hill; & we accompanied them down the creek, leaving the trail to the left. Our path lay along the top of the bank above the creek, & in a hollow of what appeared to be the old bed of a stream; at the further end was the 'Ayrshire Lass'; here we found 2 men working at a tunnel into the side of the mountain. Not yet struck the bedrock. They gave up work & led the way down the hillside into the valley to their cabin. Invited us to stay with them all night as it was already nearly dark, & too late to see the famous Hill diggings that night. We agreed, & they cooked us bacon & beans & with a small bottle of real H.B. Rum given us by John Ducie Cusheon at parting, we spent a very pleasant evening. Adam Ross, one of the two, had been a very extensive explorer along Vancouver Island & this coast. Told us 24,000 of one tribe of Indians died last year of small-pox. Turned out into the bush when attacked by the disease, & the men shot themselves & the women hanged themselves; might be seen dead by hundreds; a continual fusillade; awful cold night & only one blanket apiece.

Saturday, October 31st—Bade adieu to our miner friends & went on with Mathieson to view the Butcher & Discovery Claims on the hill; we found men at work on the Butcher, & some sinking a tunnel, others working out from the surface. Could pick out gold from the dirt about a yard below the surface; beautifully fine without quartz & deep yellow. Had all been worked by "hydraulicking," but now too cold, & sluicing used; 200 feet above creek. Old bed of a creek going at right angles into mountain; to be the great excitement next season. Lightning so termed from the Yankee expression, it being very difficult to work, & very uncertain. The lead is lost at every turn of the creek, where it passes round a point. Many claims thus found nothing. It is now supposed that the lead runs thro' the hill at these points, there having been slides which have covered over the original bed. The Hill diggings were discovered by their being at a claim below in the bed of present creek, & finding that the lead evidently did not come down the creek, but from the hill. They tunnelled into the hill to no purpose, but one day one of the boys went on to the top & scratching the earth with his knife saw gold, & on further investigating, it was found in plenty, sometimes 3 or 4 feet only below. Never more than 15 or 16; in Discovery Claim less. Went to Van Winkle for dinner, & then to Welsh Co., 2 miles on. Evans the manager not at home. His son very civil; if there is gold in the creek, they must have it, for they will prospect the whole bottom. Wheel burst with frost, stopping working of shaft; great drawback to Lightning is bed of quicksand; 25 Welshmen employed; backed by Manchester Capitalists.

Sunday, November 1st—Bade goodbye to Mr MacCaffrey & walked on to the Welsh Company's claim. Found Evans Senior at home keeping Sunday. A contrast to William's Creek. He told us that they were now prospecting in the mountains all round & had come upon what he expected would prove a valuable silver lead; no gold; expected to drop upon the "Last Chance" lead with their shaft. Provisions alone had cost $12,000 in 4 months. Had 4 pumps & were completely master of the water in the shaft, which he considered was the main point & which had been the great stumbling block to miners hitherto. Had taken up that claim on Lightning because as the mining laws at present stand the Government cannot grant a lease for a claim over 100 feet unless of ground already worked & abandoned by other miners; therefore he must either take up this large piece of abandoned ground or put himself in the hands of his men by taking up 100 feet in the name of each. But it appears there was enough vacant ground in William's Creek if the law had allowed him to lease it. We passed forward to Beaver Pass for Dinner, 10 miles from Van Winkle & from there 6 miles forward to Edward's. He has been a mate on board a merchant-man for 8 or 9 years, after that mining in Australia, came over here in '58. He is a thorough-going Englishman & gave us several amusing stories of the state of things on the first rush to this country. How he was quite alone amongst the Yankees at Boston Bar (or one of the Fraser River Bars); how they bullied him & he gave them tit for tat, they at last rolling him in a ditch & covering him with sand to make an American Citizen of him. We also heard the stories (I forget from whom) of Abbot, the successful Cariboo miner, who shied a handful of 20 dollar pieces at a large pier-glass at Victoria worth some $200, and another who, having treated all the Company in the bar room & finding no more, had all the glasses of the Establishment filled up on the counter, & swept them off with his fist! Another who in the same way being unable to find enough people to treat opened a hamper of champagne & jumped into it, thereby cutting his shins considerably. Major Downie, formerly of Downieville, California, now on William's Creek, at the Christening of Downieville set up champagne bottles in the ten pin alley & bowled at them! Most of these in fact all are in low water now. Edwards said altho' he hated Yankees, he had the greatest admiration of their energy; they opened out this country in '58 or '59, mostly Southerners; at Boston Bar some of the Yankees got up an excitement, which was agitated by the steamboat proprietor who brought such a report down to Victoria that the Governor sent up Col. Moody & a company of the Engineers in the steamer at once. Steamer stuck on the rapids & was detained a day or two, the owner drawing pay all the time; when they arrived at the place, there was a great laugh at the expense of the soldiers, the only disturbance which had occurred being between the notorious Ned McGowan & another, in which the former had blackened the eyes of the other. McGowan was fined $25, & the Officers went & had a champagne lunch with him afterwards! 2 Justices of the Peace, one at Yale & and the other at Hope, each decided the cases according as he was paid & constant appeals from one to the other.

Monday, November 2nd—A rough walk from Edward's to Cottonwood, 16 miles. Marten tracks every few yards. Milton & I treed one & fired 6 shots at him with our revolvers without effect. Dined at Smith & Ryder's, & then walked on in heavy snowstorm, to Ramsay's (Cottonwood) for the night. About 20 men there. Got plenty of blankets tho' not very clean. The same amount of snow as at William's Creek.

Tuesday, November 3rd—Very muddy trail to 8-mile house, an Irishman's who gave us a very nice dinner. Chinaman cook. Trapping martens hard; had killed a dozen with a few wretched traps near the house. From there a long 12 miles in to Quesnel mouth; where we arrived after dark; put up at Brown's where they made us very comfortable & gave us whiskey toddy as a nightcap.

Wednesday, November 4th—Steamer [*Enterprise*] stopped & hauled on to the bank—row boat going down tomorrow to Yale which will take us to Soda Creek. Numerous Chinamen keep stores here. Chinese & English signs, Kan See washing, ironing & Bakery, etc. etc. Called on Captain Done on the Steamer. Cocktails every 5 minutes, & champagne lunch afterwards. Happiest man I ever saw. Steward tells me he takes a cocktail every ten minutes when on board. Very jolly fellow. Had to give a keg of brandy to his men before they could haul the steamer on shore. Gave them a champagne dinner on being paid off today, & we heard them singing away below deck. Came in for many champagne drinks during the day. Paid $10 for passage in boat to Soda Creek, & found to our delight & surprise that we had still 3 oz. gold dust to take us forward. Talked with McBride who has been all the season up Peace River thro' the Rocky Mountains a little below Fort St. John. Gold all the way but not in paying quantities on the other side; 7 or 8 men wintering on Peace River. Coarse gold found on Nation River, one of its tributaries. An old Scotchman some 70 years old had found a fine paying claim on that branch. Describes the country as fine farming land. Mixed prairie & timber, lots of game, cariboo tracks like sheep walks, moose, mountain sheep & bears numerous. Immense quantities of fish. Fine salmon trout. Barley & potatoes grow well at Fort George. Also had long conversation with the discoverer of the Bentinck Arm route. He puts the distance from Fort Alexander to Coast at 190 miles, & brought a pack train thro' in 12 days. Lieut. Palmer followed the Indian trail & made it 270, & damned the route. This man however gives a favourable account of the country as being suitable for farming & somewhat resembling the land about Davidson's, etc. Deep Creek; bunch grass & meadow grass in abundance; 30 houses built at Bentinck Arm already [*today's Bella Coola*]. Packers have been running by that route all summer, & one man intends to get grant from Government to make a trail thro' next season.

Here at Quesnel barley & potatoes grow well. The cultivated land has been 'reserved' by Government after being preempted by owners, & no compensation yet given for improvements. Quesnel is on a large flat surrounded by a semicircular range of low hills & on the river bank.

Thursday, November 5th—"Captain" McBride got his boat, a large strongly built 6 oar, ready to start about 11 o'clock & we, together with some 40 other passengers, embarked; very crowded; no room to sit comfortably; like flock of penned sheep. He said he had taken 50 in the same boat last year, & ran thro' to Yale, where he intended to go this time if he could get sufficient passengers. It was a miserably cold, raw, cloudy November day just such as we have in England, & snowing fast, & we were dreadfully starved in spite of several whiskey bottles which came out very soon after we started, & were all emptied before we got very far. The river was unusually low, but we ran all the "riffles" successfully until we came to one below Alexandria, when McBride was induced to take the wrong side by the affirmation of a passenger that the steamer always took that course. Here we stuck fast in a tremendous stream, & could not get her off; there was therefore nothing for it but for some of the men to jump overboard & lighten the boat & help to push her off; several volunteered at once, & carried some of the passengers ashore on their backs, the water being only knee deep. One unfortunate little man got a gigantic miner on his back, & losing his footing, both fell overhead into the water & got thoroughly soused, the small fellow tumbling 3 or 4 times before he could get on his legs against the strong current. Water like ice & day cold enough. Milton & I in the most cowardly manner stuck to the ship & she was quickly lifted over the shallow & taking the drenched men on board again & wrapping them in blankets, we went on until it was almost dark, when the "Cap" suggested camping for the night. Several daredevils urged going forward, but as we were still 10 miles from Soda Creek, & the river so very dangerous, they were overruled by the more sensible, & we put ashore at a large pile of wood belonging to the steamer with which we made free to kindle some enormous fires which were kept going all night. The Captain produced plenty of bread & butter & a flitch of bacon, which with some tea went very well. Milton & I each had a blanket lent us in addition to our own one each, & he constructed a covering of pine boughs, & with my feet to the fire, & a good stock of logs to replenish it, spent a very comfortable night.

Friday, November 6th—Most of the men up before daybreak. Snowing heavily, & I kept my head under the blankets until dawn. We did not start until quite light & made Soda Creek in about an hour. There were several bad places in the river, rock sticking out in the rapids, which made us very thankful we did not try them in the dark. Had breakfast at Soda Creek, left our baggage there for the express to bring forward, & then walked quietly on to Frank Way's (Deep Creek) where we stayed the night. Found the engineer of steamer going down to winter. He told amusing story of the dodges he & Captain Thomas Wright used to work, when in a small underpowered steamer, one of the first on the Fraser running up to Yale. Had a lot of Jew traders on board & heavy freight. Could not get up a riffle. "All passengers overboard to haul at the tow line," shouts Captain Wright. Not a man would stir. "How much steam on, engineer?" shouts the Captain. "175 lbs., sir, already," replies he with great seriousness. "Then put on 25 lbs., more & blow her to h—11," cries the Captain. "Aye, aye, Sir," responds engineer; this used to be quite enough for the Jew passengers; & overboard went every man like a shot & hauled up the steamer. Thus they made up for want of power.

Saturday, November 7th—Walked forward to Davidson's (Lake Valley Farm) 14 miles. Met Todd the Canadian Horse keeper at [*Fort*] Kamloops with a Company's pack train for [*Fort*] Alexandria. Told us that . . . Martin was all right but Burgess had been blown up in the boat, only small pieces of either man or boat found; no one knew how it happened. [*Martin and Burgess were HBC employees whom Cheadle and Milton had met at Fort Kamloops.*] Matches packed next to powder kegs & perhaps thus. Poor Burgess! quiet hardworking fellow.

Davidson down in Victoria but Hudson in charge, very kind; resolve to wait here a day or two for Express.

Sunday, November 8th—Walk 3 miles down to head of William's Lake to see the farm. Only good land at bottom of perhaps a thousand acres. Some of barley sown late & small on account of drought. Earlier sown very fine. Farm only commenced in spring. Cabbages very fine; potatoes good.

Wheat sown for experiment, but looked very small, weak, & yellow. These bottoms are the only land worth cultivation in British Columbia; all the rest rocky & dry, only producing bunch grass. And the alluvial valleys are not very numerous or of large extent. Pumpkins & squashes of large size. Cattle look very fat & well. Calves bred on the place particularly good.

Monday, November 9th—Tried shooting but found no grouse; ducks too wild. Read newspapers by last Express.

Tuesday, November 10th—Took walks & talked of music with Hudson . . .

Wednesday, November 11th—Hear from men coming down that Express will be several days yet. Heigh ho; rather wearisome altho' first rate feed & cookery; nigger cook up to anything.

Thursday, November 12th—Mulatto came in with nice specimen of gold from Horse Fly Creek about 35 miles from here; one of the tributaries into lower head of Quesnel lake. Coarse scaly gold of beautiful quality. Paid tolerably well, $2 to $10 to the pan. Not many men working there.
    [*The first gold in the Cariboo was mined in June 1859 on Horse Fly Creek, today the Horsefly River, by Peter Dunlevey, Tom Manifee, Jim Sellers and Tom Moffit. While*

the men were prospecting at the junction of the Chilcotin
and Fraser Rivers, they were told by a friendly Native
named Tomaah that for generations his people had picked
up on the creek nuggets the size of beans. Tomaah then led
them some 50 miles eastward to the area.]

Friday, November 13th—On Wednesday Frank Way came
in for surgical assistance, having in a drunken row with an
Irishman had his lower lip almost bitten off, & a finger to
the bone. I stitched it up for him, making a very neat job.
Foolishly refused any fee . . . Set to work & dried the barley still out, the weather being very fine & windy, the snow
almost gone, quite hot in the sun, & slight frost at night.
September or October weather of England.

Saturday, November 14th—A number of men arrived on
way down from William's Creek. Came down in canoes.
One laden to water's edge with 14 men swamped in rough
water of first riffle 2 miles below Quesnel; 7 men lost; of the
others, 5 clung to canoe & got ashore, one was thrown on
beach by an eddy, with money & blankets all safe. Another
swam ashore, but obliged to drop his blankets containing the dust when within a few yards; 3 or 4,000 dollars
lost; 5 belonging to Prince of Wales claim. Adam Ross (in
whose cabin we stopped on Lightning Creek) told us that
his partner (who we also met there) was one of those lost
altho' a good swimmer. He delayed a day at the mouth in

order to try & get a companion to go by Bentinck Arm & thus escaped. I remember the riffle well, a tremendous rush of water & very rough so that even our large boat shipped water. Frank Way came back to have his lip redressed. Went off into a fit of laughter the other night & sutures gave way. Milk punch instituted with great success.

Sunday, November 15th—Milton & Hudson rode over to Briggs 6 miles towards Deep Creek where the latter had business. Came back seedy from bad claret. I mooned about the farm. Barley drying well.

Monday, November 16th—Frank Way came over with horses for thrashing machine. Barley thrashed out altho' very wet. Express waggon came in to our great delight. Poole very sorry he had not met us (being at Alexander when we passed in the boat), for he would have given us a waggon & pair to drive ourselves down to Yale, & we should have been in Victoria by this time. Bad luck; 18 inches snow on William's Creek; none at Quesnel Mouth.

Tuesday, November 17th—Poole the Express man had to go down to William's Lake (Mimion Ranch) 11 miles, & came back this morning. Found Gompertz (who had charge of Post Office, & constable over 7 Indians, 3 of whom are under sentence of death, & the other 4 suspected of the crime) too drunk to read the letter. A Klootcheman with him as drunk as himself. Under constable equally drunk with Sywash & Klootcheman in company. Nice state of things, eh! Bid adieu to Hudson after dinner. One fellow passenger a Captain Harrison who told us he left England 20 years ago intending to return every year since & never been able. Been all over Coast of South America, Honolulu, Australia, New Zealand. Now interested in Cariboo, & partner in proposed bed rock flume. Arrived at dark Blue Tent, 23 miles, after very cold drive. Hail storm & tremendous wind; heard trees falling all round like cannonade.

Wednesday, November 18th—Off before day light; breakfast at Anderson's 10 miles on Lake La Hache. At Bridge Creek (27 miles) by dinner; from there, leaving the mixed & open country like Davidson's which extends from Bridge Creek to Frank Way's (Deep Creek), we pass up right on to the mountain of green timber at considerable elevation which lasts for 53 miles, nearly to Junction. The road here was covered with ice, & we had to walk up the hill. One horse came down, & we had to unlimber & help up the hill by pushing behind; took us till 8 to get to 84-mile house; we had hoped to reach 74 (Loch Lomond, the old Sergeant's); very severe for horses.

Thursday, November 19th—Overslept & had breakfast before starting. Road a sheet of ice covered with a few inches of snow. Horses frequently down; had to help the waggon up the steep hills. Met Express coming up at 79-mile post & changed drivers, going forward to Loch Lomond, Sergeant McMurphy's, dined there, & afterwards only got to 59-mile house. Began to snow heavily before we got in. Man went out & shot wolf prowling round.

Friday, November 20th—Up at 5.30, starting at daybreak to 47-mile House (Clinton Cut-Off Valley) for breakfast. Fearfully cold; 6 inches of snow during night. Arrived about 10. Horses done, & our feet almost frozen. A lot of teamsters & packers at the "Hotel," drinking & one proposed as a toast "The American Eagle which whipped Great Britain, spat on France, p—d on Spain & Portugal," & —— with a brick bat afterwards. We were glad to get away from the noise. We did not get off until 3 o'clock, then had 30 miles to do. We had fine moonlight & got to Cornwall's Ranch about 9 o'clock. They have 2 houses, one wayside kept by an employee & their own farm house some ½ mile distant.

The Chinaman cook had got to bed & turned out very sulky to provide us with beefsteaks—our fellow passenger Captain Harrison would have toast which added to his ill-temper. The younger Cornwall (the elder being down at Victoria for supplies) sent word down that he would be glad to see us at the other house & Milton & I walked up there after supper. Found a tall regular First-Trinity man who received us very hospitably. Had evidently been much disappointed with the country & agriculture. He said some barley had turned out very well; the rest badly; irrigation required. Has got post holes dug for some 3 miles; land open, bunch grass country, either sand or gravel, & I feel certain will never pay for cultivation. They are now going in for Stock farming which will do well if bunch grass lasts. He took his degree in 1859; came out here April 1862.

[*In 1862 Clement F. and Henry P. Cornwall started Cornwall Ranch, which became one of the best known in the Interior. The first 150 cattle they purchased for $10 each at Coeur D'Alene, Idaho. Bringing them home "only" entailed a drive across the State of Washington, then some 200 miles up the Okanagan Valley, over the hills to swim across the Thompson River and, finally, into home pasture. The gold rush stimulated sales and the cattle were sold at a good profit.*

Two English traditions maintained by the brothers were horse racing and fox hunting. The horse races on Cornwall Flats attracted upwards of 1,000 spectators from all over BC, most arriving on horseback or by stagecoach. When English thoroughbreds failed to satisfy the sporting brothers' demands, they imported an Arabian stud.

The fox hunts—actually coyote hunts—were conducted with the same pomp and ceremony as in England. The illusion was heightened by having Natives dressed in red coats open and close gates as the boisterous hunters charged across farm and field. Every effort was made to procure the best hounds, even to having special dogs shipped around Cape Horn in sailing ships.

Ashcroft Manor, built in 1863, is an excellent example of a pioneer roadhouse. HERITAGE HOUSE

In 1862, the brothers built a flour mill and a stopping place they called Ashcroft Manor. In the days when roadside hostels were so rough and dirty that some discerning travellers preferred to sleep in the fields, Cornwall's was described as "the quietest, most comfortable hotel on the road with lots of English papers lying around the rooms." The original building also served as the first courthouse in the area, as well as a store and post office. Clement Cornwall became Lieutenant Governor of BC in 1881.

Ashcroft Manor still serves the public, although not as a hostel. It is now a museum and tea house where visitors can turn back the clock well over a century and see how travellers were accommodated in the early 1860s.]

Saturday, November 21st—Went off without disturbing our host & drove over to Cook's Ferry [*today's Spences Bridge*] for dinner. The road for 3 or 4 miles some few miles before the ferry passes round some high rocky bluffs. The dangerous trail we rode over when coming down before, the road being then not finished. It is now only 12 feet wide professedly; in many parts really much less from sliding down of the steep sides above the road partially blocking it; the pole was loose, spring broken, waggon generally very loose, traces continually coming off, no brake, heavy load (170 lbs. gold, 4 passengers & luggage) 2 small horses very tired; road very steep up to point of bluff, & then ditto down, about width of waggon, sheer descent of 600 or 700 feet into rocky bed of Thompson, perpendicular side of mountain above; a restive horse or any breakage certain destruction. Part of the road last made by the Engineers (when L. Palmer was anxious to get away to be married) was a narrow strip of loose sand, built up at the edge by loose stones which had partly given way; an awful place. We crossed carefully & safely. Arrived at Cook's Ferry for dinner, after which drove within 10 miles of Lytton; similar road but wider; same precipices & steeps; waggon pole dropped loose, fortunately when we were on the level; tied him up again.

Sunday, November 22nd—Arrived in Lytton to breakfast. Met Captain Ball again. Parson came up from Yale to hold service in the Court house, but no notice had been given,

& no congregation could be got altho' vigorous efforts were made by sending a Sywash round as bellman. Nearly all French & French Canadians in Lytton. Great hopes from Shushwap country which is described as having $60 diggings and abounding in $20 ditto.

Went forward 15 miles for night horses being too tired to do more; leaving 47 miles to do tomorrow.

Monday, November 23rd—Boston Bar to breakfast; 17 miles; quite a little town; same style of road. Had been well-to-do in river digging ore; now a miserable hole. Delayed a long time there feeding horses; reached bridge 14 miles above Yale a little after dark. On leaving here a few hundred yards the waggon completely broke down, the iron stanchions giving way and pole & cross bars tumbling to ground; on level road; wonderful luck; if this had happened on a precipice we should probably have been lost. Fortunately the other waggon belonging to Express was at the bridge with a splendid pair of horses, Smith's of Cottonwood who was taking some goods up in it. Humphreys, therefore went back for them, whilst we stayed to guard the treasure. We lighted a good fire in the road which served to amuse us until Humphreys returned with other waggon & extra horses which we hitched on in front. Humphreys had brought a bottle of brandy & was greatly exhilarated, had never driven 4 in hand before. Off we went, however we went rattling down hill along the edge of precipices at an awful pace.

Humphreys holding reins, Smith sitting beside, whipping up & passing the brandy. Milton & I were in a funk at first, but seeing that the leaders took all the turns to perfection without guiding, felt relieved & half dozed into Yale where we arrived at ½ past 10, having come the 14 miles in about 2 hours. Had supper of tough old fowls, & then turned in about 1. Canyons above Yale very fine. Large rocks stand out in the middle of river.

Tuesday, November 24th—On board 'Reliance,' having borrowed $30 from Alard, H.B. Co.'s officer in charge there. Arrived at New Westminster about 6. Called on Captain Spalding, very demonstrative. Abused Colonel Moody & told very long wearisome yarns about tigers & serpents in India. Mrs. S. vainly endeavouring to break the spell. Went on board 'Enterprise' for night in a pouring rain.

Wednesday, November 25th—Not off till 12, full of passengers. Very rough thro' Gulf of Georgia; several sick; I had to retire & assume recumbent posture to quieten sundry qualms. After became still & dined in peace. No cash left. Purser refused to take our fare, the H.B. Co. magnificently granting free passage again. Captain Mowatt came to warn me against our travelling friend Captain Harrison whom he stated was rather disreputable; a kind of male pimp from what I could make out. We reached Victoria at 6.30 & went to St. George's where we were rapturously welcomed by Mrs. Bendixen. Had bath & went to Theatre where we saw tragedy of Camille, a version of Lady of Camellias, much overdone by Mrs. Dean Hayne. Milton then adjourned to the 'Fashion' and I to bed.

Thursday, November 26th—Not up till noon! Spent day in reading papers & shopping as required much refitting. Milton went to Lyceum, I remained to Journalise & read.

Friday, November 27th—Called on Governor [*Douglas*] who kept us to dine. Begbie & Captain Martley also there. Begbie very fine, a fine tall fellow of 6 feet, well made & powerful, magnificent head, hair scanty & nearly white, with nearly black moustache & beard, full of wit. I was much taken with him. 'Sir James' was very kind, & Lady Douglas homely & good natured.

Saturday, November 28th—Invited to St. Andrews Society's dinner on Monday. Dined with Good (Governor's son-in-law, & an Official of B.C.). Played Vingt-et-un till midnight.

Sunday, November 29th—Called on the Mayor concerning steamer 'Emily Harris' for Nanaimo; to sail on Tuesday. Lascelles [*Lieutenant Commander the Honourable Horace Douglas Lascelles, seventh son of the Earl of Harewood, a naval officer at Esquimalt and a friend of Milton*] sent word we had better delay until the 'Forward' which he would take there when the next mail came in, & we decided to do so as being much pleasanter.

Monday, November 30th—Business all day with H.B. Company & our debts, etc., dining with St. Andrews Society in evening; hiring full dress from tailor. Very mild affair. Retired after set toasts & played whist soberly in Begbie's rooms till 4 a.m. Milton going round of town with Lascelles.

Tuesday, December 1—I wrote my journal & idled. Milton driving down to Esquimalt with Elwyn. Lascelles had not yet reappeared there. In evening were preparing to go to Mrs. Morse's when Milton was suddenly seized by one of his attacks without the usual premonitory symptoms & I had to wait on him all evening.

Wednesday, December 2—Had arranged to go out to Race Rocks Lighthouse with Lascelles in gunboat but tremendous wind & rain in morning, & he sent word too rough. Milton very seedy of course & in bed, & I had to remain about.

Thursday, December 3rd—Idled about, Milton being seedy & I looking after him. In evening went to dine with Dr. Walker who lives with a Mr. Passmores (any relation to the Coventrys) & young wife. Anstruther there, son of Sir Ralf, Tobey another baronet's son, Rushton of the bank, &

a German name unknown; a quiet pleasant dinner; afterwards went to the 'Fashion' where Tobey got very screwed. Heard no more of Lascelles who seems to have subsided into private life again. He sent word he was waiting to take us out to the Race Rocks today, but we, being not out of bed at the time, declined.

Friday, December 4th—Dined with the Mayor [*Thomas Harris, a huge man who weighed 300 pounds*]. ("Madame Bendixen" inveighed against the degradation of dining with 'le gros boucher'); Harris is a butcher & commenced life here by borrowing 2 sheep from the H.B. Company & selling mutton retail in a tent. The Attorney General Cary was there & ended very drunk. We sat 5 hours & never joined the ladies. Walkem, a barrister, was great in stories of Cox [*William Cox, gold commissioner, collector of customs and Justice of the Peace for the Rock Creek district*] & his "Rock Creek Justice." How he treated the thief at Hills Bar, cattle drive at Rock Creek & Mortgage case at William's Creek; he made us roar with laughter.

Epilogue

MILTON AND CHEADLE LEFT VICTORIA on December 20
by boat for Panama. Here they crossed the isthmus by
land—the Panama Canal was still some 50 years in the
future—then continued by water to England via New York.
Cheadle completed his successful book, then returned
to medicine. His career was a long and distinguished one.
He was Dean of St. Mary's Medical School from 1869 to
1873 and among the early supporters of allowing women
to study medicine. In fact, Cheadle was one of the first
professors to lecture at the London School of Medicine
for Women. In 1866, he married Anne Murgatroyd
and they had four sons. Unfortunately, Anne died at an
early age; he married again in 1884, but his second wife

also predeceased him. Dr. Cheadle died in 1910 at 75. In addition to his books, he was the author of many papers on children's health, a field in which he specialized. Lord Milton, by contrast, was fated for a short life. He lived only 13 years after their return to England, dying in 1877 at 38.

The "mere party of pleasure," as Dr. Cheadle described themselves, is commemorated by Mount Milton and Mount Cheadle between Blue River and Valemount in the North Thompson Valley. This is the region where in 1863 they were six weeks fighting through 180 miles of wilderness between Mount Robson and Fort Kamloops and almost died of starvation. Over Highway 5 the same journey is now an easy four-hour drive.

Index

About the Author

Art Downs, described as "the first of the environmental editors," was one of the forefathers of the BC publishing industry. Born in England in 1924, Art emigrated with his parents as a young child, settling in northeastern Saskatchewan. He worked in the merchant navy during the Second World War, then moved to the Quesnel River valley in the Cariboo. He became owner and editor of the *Cariboo Digest*, which evolved into *BC Outdoors*, a successful blend of history, wildlife and conservation. In 1979, Art and his wife Doris established Heritage House and began publishing books by BC writers for BC readers. He died in Surrey in 1996.

More Amazing Stories

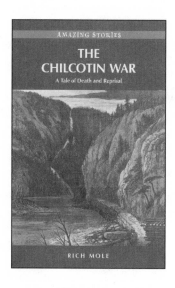

The Chilcotin War

A Tale of Death and Reprisal

Rich Mole

print ISBN 978-1-894974-96-7
ebook ISBN 978-1-926936-30-7

In 1864, a Tsilhqot'in war party killed members of a road crew carving out a mountain shortcut to the Cariboo gold creeks. Other violence followed in the tragic episode now known as the Chilcotin War, a historical drama filled with unforgettable characters. An obsessed entrepreneur who risked everything to make his dream a reality. A humiliated war chief who feared for the future of his people. A legendary trader with a secret that made him impervious to bullets. A frontier judge tormented that an official's actions might set murderers free. A new governor who faced his worst nightmare, or perhaps his greatest triumph. This is *The Chilcotin War*—a true tale of clashing cultures, greed, revenge and betrayal.

Visit heritagehouse.ca to see the entire list of books in the Amazing Stories series.

More Amazing Stories

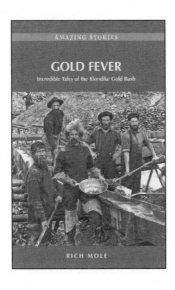

Gold Fever

Incredible Tales of the
Klondike Gold Rush

Rich Mole

print ISBN 978-1-894974-69-1
ebook ISBN 978-1-926936-21-5

In 1897, tens of thousands of would-be prospectors flooded into the
Yukon in search of instant wealth during the Klondike Gold Rush. In
this historical tale of mayhem and obsession, characters like prospectors
George Carmack and Skookum Jim, Skagway gangster Soapy Smith and
Mountie Sam Steele come to life. Enduring savage weather, unforgiving
terrain, violence and starvation, a lucky few made their fortune, and
some just as quickly lost it. The lure of the North is still irresistible in
this exciting account of a fabled era of Canadian history.

Visit heritagehouse.ca to see the entire list of books in the Amazing Stories series.

More Amazing Stories

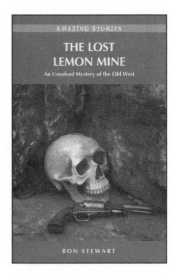

The Lost Lemon Mine

An Unsolved Mystery
of the Old West

Ron Stewart

print ISBN 978-1-926613-99-4
ebook ISBN 978-1-926936-66-6

In 1870, so the story goes, a prospector named Lemon and his partner, Blackjack, found gold in the rugged mountains of southwestern Alberta or southeastern British Columbia. Shortly after, Blackjack died at Lemon's hand. The distraught Lemon left the scene of the murder and never recovered his senses—or his gold. But is this what really happened? Ron Stewart digs into the often-conflicting historical evidence behind the intriguing legend of the Lost Lemon Mine in an attempt to separate fact from folklore and shed light on one of the most enduring unsolved mysteries of the Canadian West.

Visit heritagehouse.ca to see the entire list of books in the Amazing Stories series.